Mocktails Made Simple

Over 100+ Alcohol-Free Recipes to Enjoy Every Sip

Victoria O. Foster

Copyright

This book is copyright © 2025 by Victoria O. Foster. All rights are reserved. Any unauthorized reproduction, sharing, or distribution of this work, in part or in its entirety, is strictly prohibited. This includes any form of digital or analog replica, such as photocopying, recording, or information storage and retrieval systems, except as permitted under sections of copyright law for brief quotations in a review.

Legal Disclaimer

The material presented in this book is intended for informational purposes only. No warranty, express or implied, on the quality, precision, or suitability for a particular purpose of the content is offered. The author shall not be held responsible for any direct, consequential, or incidental damages arising from using or misusing any information herein. While every effort has been made to ensure the accuracy of the material in this book, neither the author nor the publisher accepts responsibility for any mistakes, inaccuracies, or omissions. If you need professional advice, please consult a qualified professional.

Your purchase and use of this book indicate your acceptance of these terms and conditions.

Table of Contents

Welcome to the World of Incredible Alcohol-Free Mocktails! 5
Why Mocktails Matter 6
Setting Up Your Mocktail Bar 7
Fruity Delights 8
    Tropical Paradise Punch 9
    Berry Burst Bliss 9
    Citrus Sunrise Sparkler 10
    Mango Magic Mojito 10
    Strawberry Lemonade Splash 11
    Watermelon Wonder Cooler 11
    Raspberry Lime Fizz 12
    Peach Passion Punch 12
    Kiwi Kiss Refresher 13
    Pomegranate Power Sip 13
    Pineapple Breeze Mocktail 14
    Blueberry Basil Spritzer 14
Exotic Blends 15
    Coconut Lychee Cooler 16
    Dragonfruit Dream Spritz 16
    Mango Tamarind Elixir 17
    Pineapple Ginger Zest 17
    Passionfruit Paradise Punch 18
    Thai Basil Lime Cooler 18
    Guava Hibiscus Fizz 19
    Papaya Mint Mojito 19
    Spiced Mango Sunrise 20
    Cucumber Coconut Bliss 20
    Starfruit Citrus Sparkler 21
    Tamarind Tangerine Tonic 21
Low-Calorie Mocktails 22
    Skinny Lemon Ginger Fizz 23
    Light & Lush Lime Spritz 23
    Cranberry Orange Cooler 24
    Low-Cal Cucumber Mint Refresher 24
    Berry Light Sparkler 25
    Citrus Cloud Elixir 25
    Watermelon Mint Delight 26
    Aloe Vera Lemon Cooler 26
    Green Tea Lime Sparkle 27
    Hibiscus Slim Sip 27
    Grapefruit Basil Bliss 28
    Skinny Peachy Punch 28
Savory Sips 29
    Tomato Basil Cooler 30
    Cucumber Dill Refresher 30
    Spiced Carrot Ginger Spark 31
    Bloody Mary Mocktail 31
    Avocado Cilantro Smooth Sip 32
    Jalapeño Lime Zest 32
    Beetroot Lemon Spritz 33
    Celery Salt & Lemon Fizz 33
    Turmeric Tamarind Tonic 34
    Sweet Potato Maple Swirl 34
    Smoky Paprika Citrus Splash 35
    Pickled Cucumber Cooler 35
Energizing Boosts 36
    Matcha Mint Cooler 37
    Espresso Orange Twist 37
    Beet Ginger Booster 38
    Coconut Espresso Spark 38
    Lemon Chia Energizer 39
    Green Tea Citrus Charge 39
    Guarana Berry Bliss 40
    Ginseng Grapefruit Fizz 40
    Mango Protein Punch 41
    Acai Berry Refresher 41
    Pineapple Spirulina Zest 42
    Turmeric Honey Glow 42
Timeless Classics 43

Virgin Mojito	44
Non-Alcoholic Piña Colada	44
Classic Shirley Temple	45
Faux Sangria Sparkle	45
Virgin Mary	46
Nojito (Alcohol-Free Mojito)	46
Classic Lemon Spritzer	47
Non-Alcoholic Margarita	47
Alcohol-Free Cosmo Cooler	48
Mimosa Mocktail	48
Apple Cider Spritz	49
Non-Alcoholic Martini Twist	49
Dessert-Inspired Drinks	**50**
Chocolate Mint Bliss	51
Vanilla Bean Cream Soda	51
Strawberry Cheesecake Shake	52
Key Lime Pie Refresher	52
Salted Caramel Spritz	53
Banoffee Cream Cooler	53
Cinnamon Roll Elixir	54
Tiramisu Mocktail	54
Almond Joy Refresher	55
Raspberry Chocolate Bliss	55
S'mores Shake Fizz	56
Coconut Cream Delight	56
Herbal Infusions	**57**
Lavender Lemonade Cooler	58
Rosemary Citrus Sparkler	58
Mint & Honey Elixir	59
Basil Berry Bliss	59
Chamomile Citrus Dream	60
Sage & Pear Refresher	60
Thyme Pineapple Spritz	61
Hibiscus Rose Cooler	61
Eucalyptus Lime Tonic	62
Peppermint Peach Fizz	62
Lemon Verbena Delight	63
Ginger Lemongrass Splash	63
Mocktails For Kids	**64**
Fizzy Berry Lemonade	65
Rainbow Fruit Punch	65
Strawberry Banana Fizz	66
Cotton Candy Cloud Cooler	66
Blueberry Bubble Mocktail	67
Tropical Unicorn Spritz	67
Watermelon Wonder Splash	68
Chocolate Milkshake Spritzer	68
Apple Pie Sparkle	69
Kiwi Melon Magic	69
Grape Galaxy Fizz	70
Orange Cream Dream	70
Conclusion	**71**
Index	**72**

Welcome to the World of Incredible Alcohol-Free Mocktails!

If you're looking for delicious, alcohol-free drinks that are easy to make and even easier to enjoy, you've come to the right place. Mocktails have become more than just an alternative to traditional cocktails — they are a flavorful and refreshing choice for anyone who wants to sip something special without the alcohol.

In this book, Mocktails Made Simple, you'll find over 100 easy-to-follow recipes designed for every occasion. Whether you're unwinding after a long day, celebrating with friends, or just looking for a fun and tasty drink, this collection has something for you.

Forget complicated cocktail recipes with hard-to-find ingredients! This book focuses on simple pleasures — fresh flavors, easy techniques, and ingredients that are already in your kitchen or can be easily found at your local grocery store.

So, grab your glass, gather some fresh ingredients, and let's embark on a delicious journey into the art of crafting mocktails!

Why Mocktails Matter

Refreshing, Fun, and Alcohol-Free

Mocktails aren't just a substitute for alcoholic drinks — they are an experience in themselves. Whether you're hosting a party, looking for a healthier alternative, or simply want to enjoy a sophisticated drink without the buzz, mocktails bring flavor, creativity, and variety to the table.

The Benefits of Mocktails:

✅ Healthier Choices – Avoid the negative effects of alcohol while still enjoying a beautifully crafted drink.
✅ Inclusivity – Mocktails are perfect for everyone, including kids, pregnant women, and those who choose not to drink alcohol.
✅ Creative & Fun – With endless flavor combinations, you can explore fresh ingredients, bold infusions, and stunning presentations.
✅ No Hangovers – Enjoy delicious drinks without the next-day regret!

Mocktails aren't just an alternative — they are a celebration of fresh ingredients and vibrant flavors that anyone can enjoy.

Setting Up Your Mocktail Bar

Essential Tools, Glassware, and Garnishes

Before you start mixing, it's important to have the right tools and ingredients to create perfect mocktails. The good news? You don't need a fancy setup—just a few essentials will set you up for success.

Basic Tools You'll Need:
- 🍹 Pitcher – Perfect for mixing and serving large batches of mocktails.
- 🍹 Blender or Stick Blender – Ideal for smooth, creamy drinks and fruit-based blends.
- 🍹 Citrus Press or Juicer – Extracts fresh juice from lemons, limes, oranges, and grapefruit.
- 🍹 Vegetable Juicer – Great for vibrant juices from fresh fruits and veggies.
- 🍹 Strainer – Helps remove pulp, seeds, or herb bits for a smooth finish.
- 🍹 Cheesecloth or Coffee Filter (Optional) – For ultra-smooth syrups and infusions.

Glassware & Presentation:
- 🥂 Highball Glass – Perfect for tall, refreshing mocktails.
- 🍸 Martini Glass – Ideal for elegant and stylish drinks.
- 🍹 Mason Jar – A rustic touch for casual gatherings.
- 🥤 Tumbler – Versatile and great for everyday mocktails.

Garnishes & Enhancements:
- ✨ Fresh herbs (mint, basil, rosemary)
- ✨ Citrus slices (lemon, lime, orange)
- ✨ Berries & tropical fruits
- ✨ Edible flowers
- ✨ Ice cubes infused with fruit or herbs

With these essentials, you're ready to create mocktails that look as good as they taste!

Fruity Delights

TROPICAL PARADISE PUNCH

4 SERVINGS | 10 MINUTES | 0 MINUTES

Ingredients:
- 2 cups Pineapple Juice
- 1 cup Orange Juice
- 1 cup Mango Nectar
- 1/2 cup Coconut Water
- 1/4 cup Lime Juice
- 1/4 cup Grenadine Syrup
- Ice cubes, as needed
- Pineapple slices and mint leaves for garnish

Directions:
1. Combine pineapple juice, orange juice, mango nectar, coconut water, and lime juice in a large pitcher.
2. Stir in the grenadine syrup gently to create a beautiful gradient effect.
3. Fill serving glasses with ice cubes.
4. Pour the mixture over the ice and garnish with pineapple slices and mint leaves.
5. Serve immediately and let the tropical flavors whisk you away!

Nutritional Information:
Calories: 150, Protein: 1g, Carbohydrates: 37g, Fat: 0g, Fiber: 1g, Cholesterol: 0 mg, Sodium: 20 mg, Potassium: 370 mg

BERRY BURST BLISS

2 SERVINGS | 10 MINUTES | 0 MINUTES

Ingredients:
- 1 cup mixed berries (fresh or frozen)
- 1 cup sparkling water
- 1/2 cup pineapple juice
- 1 tablespoon fresh lemon juice
- 1 teaspoon honey (optional)
- Ice cubes

Directions:
1. Combine the mixed berries, pineapple juice, and lemon juice in a blender.
2. Blend until smooth and the berries are completely pureed.
3. Strain the mixture through a strainer to remove the pulp and seeds.
4. Add honey to the strained juice, if using, and stir until dissolved.
5. Divide the mixture between two serving glasses filled with ice cubes.
6. Top each glass with sparkling water and gently stir.
7. Garnish with a fresh berry or a lemon slice, if desired, and serve immediately.

Nutritional Information:
Calories: 80, Protein: 1g, Carbohydrates: 20g, Fat: 0g, Fiber: 3g, Cholesterol: 0mg, Sodium: 5mg, Potassium: 150mg

Moctails

CITRUS SUNRISE SPARKLER

2 SERVINGS   10 MINUTES   0 MINUTES

Ingredients:

- 1 cup Fresh Orange Juice
- 1/2 cup Sparkling Water
- 2 tablespoons Lemon Juice
- 1 tablespoon Honey (or Agave Syrup for a vegan option)
- 4-5 Fresh Mint Leaves
- Ice Cubes
- Orange Slices and Mint Sprigs for Garnish

Directions:

1. In a cocktail shaker, combine fresh orange juice, lemon juice, honey (or agave syrup), and mint leaves.
2. Add a handful of ice cubes, seal the shaker, and shake vigorously for about 20 seconds.
3. Strain the mixture into tall glasses filled with ice cubes.
4. Top each glass with sparkling water, stirring gently to combine.
5. Garnish with orange slices and mint sprigs before serving.

Nutritional Information:

Calories: 90, Protein: 1g, Carbohydrates: 24g, Fat: 0g, Fiber: 1g, Cholesterol: 0mg, Sodium: 5mg, Potassium: 300mg

MANGO MAGIC MOJITO

2 SERVINGS   10 MINUTES   0 MINUTES

Ingredients:

- 1 cup fresh mango, diced
- 12 fresh mint leaves
- 2 tablespoons lime juice
- 2 tablespoons honey (or agave syrup)
- 1 cup club soda
- Ice cubes
- Lime slices and mint sprigs, for garnish

Directions:

1. In a cocktail shaker, muddle the mango pieces and mint leaves until well combined.
2. Add lime juice and honey to the mixture, and give it a gentle shake to mix.
3. Fill two tall glasses with ice cubes and strain the mango mint mixture evenly into the glasses.
4. Top each glass with club soda and stir gently to combine.
5. Garnish with lime slices and mint sprigs before serving.

Nutritional Information:

Calories: 95, Protein: 1g, Carbohydrates: 24g, Fat: 0g, Fiber: 2g, Cholesterol: 0mg, Sodium: 20mg, Potassium: 180mg

Moctails

STRAWBERRY LEMONADE SPLASH

🍽️ 4 SERVINGS   ⏱️ 10 MINUTES   🕐 0 MINUTES

Ingredients:

- 2 cups fresh strawberries, hulled
- 1 cup freshly squeezed lemon juice (about 4-6 lemons)
- 1/2 cup honey or agave syrup
- 3 cups cold sparkling water
- Ice cubes
- Fresh mint leaves, for garnish (optional)

Directions:

1. In a blender, combine the strawberries, lemon juice, and honey. Blend until smooth.
2. Strain the mixture through a fine-mesh sieve into a pitcher to remove the seeds and pulp.
3. Add the sparkling water to the pitcher, stirring well to combine the flavors.
4. Fill glasses with ice cubes, then pour the strawberry lemonade mixture over the ice.
5. Garnish each glass with fresh mint leaves if desired, and serve immediately.

Nutritional Information:

Calories: 85, Protein: 1g, Carbohydrates: 22g, Fat: 0g, Fiber: 2g, Cholesterol: 0mg, Sodium: 5mg, Potassium: 180mg

WATERMELON WONDER COOLER

🍽️ 4 SERVINGS   ⏱️ 10 MINUTES   🕐 0 MINUTES

Ingredients:

- 4 cups watermelon, cubed
- 1/4 cup fresh lime juice
- 2 tablespoons honey (or agave syrup)
- 1 cup coconut water
- Ice cubes, as needed
- Fresh mint leaves, for garnish

Directions:

1. In a blender, combine watermelon cubes and blend until smooth.
2. Strain the watermelon juice through a fine-mesh sieve into a pitcher to remove pulp.
3. Stir in lime juice, honey, and coconut water until well mixed.
4. Fill serving glasses with ice cubes and pour the watermelon mixture over the ice.
5. Garnish with fresh mint leaves before serving.

Nutritional Information:

Calories: 55, Protein: 1g, Carbohydrates: 14g, Fat: 0g, Fiber: 1g, Cholesterol: 0 mg, Sodium: 15 mg, Potassium: 200 mg

Moctails

RASPBERRY LIME FIZZ

🍽 2 SERVINGS   ⏱ 10 MINUTES   🕐 0 MINUTES

Ingredients:

- 1/2 cup Fresh Raspberries
- 1 Lime, juiced
- 1 tbsp Honey (or agave syrup for vegan option)
- 1 cup Club Soda
- Ice cubes
- Lime slices and raspberries for garnish

Directions:

1. In the shaker, muddle the fresh raspberries with lime juice and honey until well combined and the raspberries are pulpy.
2. Add ice cubes to the shaker and shake vigorously for about 15 seconds.
3. Strain the mixture into two glasses filled with ice cubes, dividing it evenly.
4. Top each glass with club soda, stirring gently to combine.
5. Garnish with lime slices and fresh raspberries for an extra pop of color.

Nutritional Information:

Calories: 60, Protein: 0.5g, Carbohydrates: 16g, Fat: 0g, Fiber: 3g, Cholesterol: 0mg, Sodium: 10mg, Potassium: 140mg

PEACH PASSION PUNCH

🍽 4 SERVINGS   ⏱ 10 MINUTES   🕐 0 MINUTES

Ingredients:

- 2 cups fresh peach slices
- 1 cup orange juice
- 1 1/2 cups sparkling water
- 1 tablespoon lime juice
- 1 tablespoon honey (optional)
- Ice cubes
- Fresh mint leaves for garnish

Directions:

1. Combine fresh peach slices and orange juice in a blender until smooth.
2. Pour the peach mixture into a pitcher and stir in lime juice and honey.
3. Add sparkling water to the pitcher; mix gently with a wooden spoon.
4. Fill glasses with ice cubes and pour the mocktail mixture over the ice.
5. Garnish with fresh mint leaves and serve immediately.

Nutritional Information:

Calories: 85, Protein: 1g, Carbohydrates: 21g, Fat: 0g, Fiber: 2g, Cholesterol: 0 mg, Sodium: 5 mg, Potassium: 320 mg

Mocktails

KIWI KISS REFRESHER

2 SERVINGS — **10 MINUTES** — **0 MINUTES**

Ingredients:

- 3 ripe kiwis, peeled and diced
- 1 tablespoon lime juice
- 1/4 cup fresh mint leaves
- 1 cup sparkling water
- 1 tablespoon honey (optional, adjust to taste)
- Ice cubes as needed

Directions:

1. In a blender, combine the diced kiwis and lime juice. Blend until smooth.
2. Pour the kiwi-lime mixture through a fine mesh strainer to remove seeds, if desired.
3. In a glass or cocktail shaker, muddle the mint leaves gently to release their aroma.
4. Add the strained kiwi mixture and honey to the glass or shaker, and stir or shake until well combined.
5. Fill two glasses with ice cubes and divide the mixture between them.
6. Top each glass with sparkling water, stirring gently to combine.
7. Garnish with additional mint leaves and kiwi slices, if desired.

Nutritional Information:

Calories: 85, Protein: 1g, Carbohydrates: 21g, Fat: 0g, Fiber: 3g, Cholesterol: 0mg, Sodium: 10mg, Potassium: 350mg

POMEGRANATE POWER SIP

2 SERVINGS — **10 MINUTES** — **0 MINUTES**

Ingredients:

- 1 cup pomegranate juice
- 1/2 cup orange juice, freshly squeezed
- 1/4 cup sparkling water
- 1 tablespoon lemon juice, freshly squeezed
- 1 tablespoon honey
- Ice cubes
- Pomegranate seeds and mint leaves, for garnish

Directions:

1. In a blender, combine pomegranate juice, orange juice, lemon juice, and honey. Blend until smooth and honey is fully dissolved.
2. Fill a cocktail shaker halfway with ice cubes.
3. Pour the blended mixture into the shaker and add the sparkling water. Seal and shake vigorously for about 15 seconds.
4. Strain the mocktail into two chilled glasses filled with ice cubes.
5. Garnish with pomegranate seeds and a sprig of mint. Serve immediately and enjoy!

Nutritional Information:

Calories: 120, Protein: 1g, Carbohydrates: 30g, Fat: 0g, Fiber: 1g, Cholesterol: 0mg, Sodium: 10mg, Potassium: 280mg

Mocktails

PINEAPPLE BREEZE MOCKTAIL

2 SERVINGS | 10 MINUTES | 0 MINUTES

Ingredients:

- 1 cup fresh pineapple chunks
- 1/2 cup coconut water
- 1 tablespoon fresh lime juice
- 5-6 fresh mint leaves
- 1 teaspoon honey (optional)
- Ice cubes
- Lime slices and mint sprigs for garnish

Directions:

1. Combine pineapple chunks, coconut water, lime juice, and mint leaves in a blender.
2. Blend until smooth, ensuring the mixture is well-combined.
3. Strain the mixture into a pitcher to remove any pulp, if desired.
4. Sweeten with honey, adding more if preferred.
5. Pour into serving glasses over ice cubes.
6. Garnish with a slice of lime and a sprig of mint before serving.

Nutritional Information:

Calories: 80, Protein: 1g, Carbohydrates: 20g, Fat: 0g, Fiber: 2g, Cholesterol: 0mg, Sodium: 25mg, Potassium: 220mg

BLUEBERRY BASIL SPRITZER

4 SERVINGS | 10 MINUTES | 0 MINUTES

Ingredients:

- 1 cup fresh blueberries
- 1/4 cup fresh basil leaves
- 1 tablespoon honey (optional, can adjust based on sweetness)
- 1 lime, juiced
- 3 cups sparkling water
- Ice cubes

Directions:

1. Place the blueberries and basil leaves into a blender. Blend until smooth.
2. Strain the blended mixture into a pitcher to remove solids.
3. Stir in honey and lime juice until well mixed.
4. Add sparkling water, and gently stir to combine.
5. Fill glasses with ice cubes and pour the spritzer over the ice.
6. Garnish with additional basil leaves or blueberries if desired. Serve chilled.

Nutritional Information:

Calories: 35, Protein: 0.5g, Carbohydrates: 9g, Fat: 0g, Fiber: 2g, Cholesterol: 0 mg, Sodium: 4 mg, Potassium: 75 mg

Moctails

Exotic Blends

COCONUT LYCHEE COOLER

2 SERVINGS　　10 MINUTES　　0 MINUTES

Ingredients:

- 1 cup Coconut Milk
- 1/2 cup Lychee Juice (from canned lychees)
- 1/4 cup Fresh Lime Juice
- 1 tablespoon Simple Syrup
- Ice Cubes
- Lychee Fruit (for garnish)
- Mint Leaves (for garnish)

Directions:

1. In a blender, combine coconut milk, lychee juice, fresh lime juice, and simple syrup.
2. Add a handful of ice cubes to the mixture and blend until smooth.
3. Pour the blend into a cocktail shaker filled with ice and shake vigorously.
4. Strain into two glasses filled with fresh ice.
5. Garnish with lychee fruit and mint leaves.

Nutritional Information:

Calories: 130, Protein: 1g, Carbohydrates: 23g, Fat: 5g, Fiber: 1g, Cholesterol: 0 mg, Sodium: 30 mg, Potassium: 200 mg

DRAGONFRUIT DREAM SPRITZ

2 SERVINGS　　10 MINUTES　　0 MINUTES

Ingredients:

- 1 cup dragonfruit, peeled and chopped
- 1/2 cup coconut water
- 1 tablespoon lime juice
- 1 tablespoon honey
- 1/2 cup sparkling water
- Fresh mint leaves for garnish
- Ice cubes

Directions:

1. Blend dragonfruit and coconut water until smooth.
2. In a cocktail shaker, muddle mint leaves to release their aroma.
3. Add lime juice, honey, and ice cubes to the shaker, then pour in the dragonfruit mixture.
4. Shake well until all ingredients are combined and chilled.
5. Strain into two tall glasses over ice.
6. Top each with sparkling water and garnish with a mint leaf.

Nutritional Information:

Calories: 80, Protein: 1g, Carbohydrates: 20g, Fat: 0g, Fiber: 3g, Cholesterol: 0 mg, Sodium: 40 mg, Potassium: 200 mg

Moctails

MANGO TAMARIND ELIXIR

🍽 4 SERVINGS   ⏱ 10 MINUTES   🕐 0 MINUTES

Ingredients:
- 2 cups fresh mango, diced
- 1/4 cup tamarind paste
- 2 tablespoons honey
- 1 cup coconut water
- 1 tablespoon lime juice
- Ice cubes, as needed
- Fresh mint leaves, for garnish

Directions:
1. Combine diced mango, tamarind paste, honey, coconut water, and lime juice in a blender.
2. Blend until smooth and all ingredients are well incorporated.
3. Strain the mixture through a sieve into a mixing bowl to remove any pulp or fibers.
4. Fill serving glasses with ice cubes.
5. Pour the strained mixture over the ice and garnish with fresh mint leaves.
6. Serve immediately and enjoy the tropical escape!

Nutritional Information:
Calories: 110, Protein: 1g, Carbohydrates: 25g, Fat: 0g, Fiber: 2g, Cholesterol: 0 mg, Sodium: 20 mg, Potassium: 300 mg

PINEAPPLE GINGER ZEST

🍽 4 SERVINGS   ⏱ 10 MINUTES   🕐 0 MINUTES

Ingredients:
- 2 cups fresh pineapple chunks
- 1 tablespoon fresh ginger, grated
- 1 tablespoon honey
- 1 cup coconut water
- 1 tablespoon lime juice
- Ice cubes
- Pineapple slices and mint sprigs for garnish

Directions:
1. Add the pineapple chunks and grated ginger to a blender.
2. Pour in the honey, coconut water, and lime juice. Blend until smooth.
3. Strain the mixture through a fine mesh strainer into a pitcher to remove pulp.
4. Fill glasses with ice cubes and pour the strained mocktail over the ice.
5. Garnish with pineapple slices and mint sprigs before serving.

Nutritional Information:
Calories: 80, Protein: 1g, Carbohydrates: 20g, Fat: 0g, Fiber: 2g, Cholesterol: 0mg, Sodium: 10mg, Potassium: 200mg

Moctails

PASSIONFRUIT PARADISE PUNCH

🍽 4 SERVINGS   ⏱ 10 MINUTES   ⏲ 0 MINUTES

Ingredients:

- 1 cup Passionfruit Juice
- 1 cup Pineapple Juice
- 1/2 cup Orange Juice
- 1/4 cup Lime Juice
- 1 cup Sparkling Water
- 1 tablespoon Honey or Agave Syrup (optional)
- Ice Cubes
- Passionfruit Slices and Mint Leaves for garnish

Directions:

1. In a mixing pitcher, combine the passionfruit juice, pineapple juice, orange juice, and lime juice.
2. Stir in the honey or agave syrup if sweetness is desired.
3. Add sparkling water to the juice mixture and gently stir to combine.
4. Fill serving glasses with ice cubes and pour the mocktail over the ice.
5. Garnish each glass with passionfruit slices and mint leaves.
6. Serve immediately, and enjoy your tropical escape!

Nutritional Information:

Calories: 75, Protein: 1g, Carbohydrates: 18g, Fat: 0g, Fiber: 0g, Cholesterol: 0mg, Sodium: 5mg, Potassium: 250mg

THAI BASIL LIME COOLER

🍽 2 SERVINGS   ⏱ 10 MINUTES   ⏲ 0 MINUTES

Ingredients:

- 1/4 cup Fresh Thai Basil Leaves
- 1/2 cup Freshly Squeezed Lime Juice
- 2 tablespoons Honey or Agave Nectar
- 1 cup Coconut Water
- 1/2 cup Crushed Ice
- Lime Slices, for garnish
- Thai Basil Sprigs, for garnish

Directions:

1. Combine Thai basil leaves, lime juice, and honey in a blender. Blend until the basil is finely chopped and well mixed.
2. Add coconut water and blend again briefly to combine.
3. Fill a shaker with crushed ice and pour the blended mixture over the ice. Shake well to chill.
4. Strain the mixture into two glasses filled with fresh ice.
5. Garnish with lime slices and Thai basil sprigs. Serve immediately.

Nutritional Information:

Calories: 70, Protein: 0g, Carbohydrates: 18g, Fat: 0g, Fiber: 1g, Cholesterol: 0 mg, Sodium: 40 mg, Potassium: 120 mg

Moctails

GUAVA HIBISCUS FIZZ

4 SERVINGS   **10 MINUTES**   **0 MINUTES**

Ingredients:

- 2 cups guava juice
- 1 cup hibiscus tea, brewed and chilled
- 1/2 cup sparkling water
- 2 tablespoons lime juice
- 1 tablespoon agave syrup
- Ice cubes, as needed
- Fresh mint leaves, for garnish

Directions:

1. Brew hibiscus tea according to instructions and chill in the refrigerator.
2. Blend guava juice, hibiscus tea, lime juice, and agave syrup until smooth.
3. Strain the mixture into a mixing pitcher to remove any pulp or tea particles.
4. Stir in the sparkling water to add a fizzy touch.
5. Pour the mocktail into glasses over ice cubes.
6. Garnish with fresh mint leaves and serve immediately.

Nutritional Information:

Calories: 80, Protein: 0g, Carbohydrates: 20g, Fat: 0g, Fiber: 1g, Cholesterol: 0mg, Sodium: 10mg, Potassium: 150mg

PAPAYA MINT MOJITO

2 SERVINGS   **10 MINUTES**   **0 MINUTES**

Ingredients:

- 1 cup ripe papaya, peeled and diced
- 10 fresh mint leaves
- 1 tablespoon honey (optional)
- 1 tablespoon lime juice
- 1 cup soda water
- Ice cubes

Directions:

1. In a blender, combine the diced papaya, lime juice, and honey; blend until smooth.
2. Use a muddler to gently crush the mint leaves in the bottom of two glasses to release their flavor.
3. Strain the papaya mixture into the glasses over the mint, dividing evenly.
4. Fill the glasses with ice cubes and top with soda water.
5. Stir gently to combine, and garnish with a sprig of mint. Serve immediately.

Nutritional Information:

Calories: 70, Protein: 1g, Carbohydrates: 18g, Fat: 0.2g, Fiber: 2g, Cholesterol: 0mg, Sodium: 5mg, Potassium: 220mg

Moctails

SPICED MANGO SUNRISE

2 SERVINGS   10 MINUTES   0 MINUTES

Ingredients:

- 1 cup fresh mango chunks
- 1/2 cup orange juice
- 1/2 teaspoon ground cinnamon
- 1/4 teaspoon ground cardamom
- 1 tablespoon lime juice
- 1 tablespoon honey (or agave syrup for a vegan option)
- 1/4 cup sparkling water
- Ice cubes
- Mango slice and cinnamon stick for garnish

Directions:

1. Combine mango chunks, orange juice, cinnamon, cardamom, lime juice, and honey in a blender; blend until smooth.
2. Fill the cocktail shaker halfway with ice cubes and pour the mango mixture in.
3. Shake well and strain the mixture into two glasses filled with ice cubes.
4. Top each glass with sparkling water and stir gently.
5. Garnish with a mango slice and a cinnamon stick before serving.

Nutritional Information:

Calories: 130, Protein: 1g, Carbohydrates: 34g, Fat: 0.5g, Fiber: 3g, Cholesterol: 0mg, Sodium: 3mg, Potassium: 330mg

CUCUMBER COCONUT BLISS

4 SERVINGS   10 MINUTES   0 MINUTES

Ingredients:

- 1 large cucumber, peeled and chopped
- 1 cup coconut milk
- 1 tablespoon lime juice
- 1 tablespoon honey or agave syrup
- 1 cup chilled sparkling water
- Ice cubes
- Mint leaves for garnish (optional)

Directions:

1. Place cucumber, coconut milk, lime juice, and honey in a blender. Blend until smooth.
2. Strain the mixture into a pitcher to remove any pulp.
3. Add the chilled sparkling water to the pitcher and stir gently.
4. Fill glasses with ice cubes and pour the mocktail over the ice.
5. Garnish with mint leaves if desired and serve immediately.

Nutritional Information:

Calories: 90, Protein: 1g, Carbohydrates: 10g, Fat: 4g, Fiber: 1g, Cholesterol: 0mg, Sodium: 25mg, Potassium: 150mg

Moctails

STARFRUIT CITRUS SPARKLER

🍽 2 SERVINGS   ⏱ 10 MINUTES   🕐 0 MINUTES

Ingredients:

- 1 ripe starfruit, sliced
- 1 orange, juiced
- 1 lime, juiced
- 1 cup sparkling water
- 1 tablespoon honey (optional)
- Ice cubes
- Starfruit slices and lime wedges for garnish

Directions:

1. Blend the sliced starfruit with orange and lime juices until smooth.
2. Strain the mixture to remove pulp and seeds.
3. Pour the strained juice into a glass and add honey, stirring until dissolved if desired.
4. Fill the glass with ice cubes and top with sparkling water.
5. Gently stir to combine flavors.
6. Garnish with starfruit slices and lime wedges. Serve immediately and enjoy.

Nutritional Information:

Calories: 45, Protein: 1g, Carbohydrates: 11g, Fat: 0g, Fiber: 2g, Cholesterol: 0mg, Sodium: 6mg, Potassium: 207mg

TAMARIND TANGERINE TONIC

🍽 2 SERVINGS   ⏱ 10 MINUTES   🕐 5 MINUTES

Ingredients:

- 2 tbsp tamarind paste
- 1 cup fresh tangerine juice
- 1 cup sparkling water
- 1 tbsp honey or agave syrup
- 1 tsp freshly grated ginger
- Ice cubes
- Tangerine slices and mint leaves for garnish

Directions:

1. In a shaker, combine tamarind paste, tangerine juice, honey, and grated ginger.
2. Fill the shaker with ice and shake vigorously for about 20 seconds.
3. Strain the mixture into two glasses filled with ice.
4. Top each glass with sparkling water and stir gently.
5. Garnish with tangerine slices and mint leaves.

Nutritional Information:

Calories: 90, Protein: 1g, Carbohydrates: 23g, Fat: 0g, Fiber: 2g, Cholesterol: 0 mg, Sodium: 10 mg, Potassium: 200 mg

Moctails

Low-Calorie Mocktails

SKINNY LEMON GINGER FIZZ

2 SERVINGS   **5 MINUTES**   **0 MINUTES**

Ingredients:

- 1 cup sparkling water
- 1/4 cup fresh lemon juice
- 1 teaspoon grated fresh ginger
- 1 teaspoon honey or agave syrup (optional for sweetness)
- Ice cubes
- Lemon slices and mint leaves for garnish

Directions:

1. In a cocktail shaker, combine the fresh lemon juice and grated ginger.
2. Add honey or agave syrup if you prefer a touch of sweetness.
3. Fill the shaker with ice cubes and pour in the sparkling water.
4. Shake gently to mix all ingredients and chill the mixture.
5. Strain into two glasses filled with ice.
6. Garnish with lemon slices and mint leaves for a refreshing look.

Nutritional Information:

Calories: 22, Protein: 0g, Carbohydrates: 6g, Fat: 0g, Fiber: 0g, Cholesterol: 0 mg, Sodium: 5 mg, Potassium: 35 mg

LIGHT & LUSH LIME SPRITZ

2 SERVINGS   **5 MINUTES**   **0 MINUTES**

Ingredients:

- 1 cup Sparkling Water
- 1/2 cup Fresh Squeezed Lime Juice
- 1 tbsp Honey or Agave Syrup
- 2 slices Fresh Lime, for garnish
- Ice Cubes, as needed
- Fresh Mint Leaves, for garnish

Directions:

1. Juice the limes to obtain 1/2 cup of fresh lime juice.
2. In a measuring cup, mix the lime juice with honey or agave syrup until fully dissolved.
3. Fill two tall glasses with ice cubes and evenly pour the lime mixture over the ice.
4. Top each glass with sparkling water, stirring gently to combine.
5. Garnish with lime slices and fresh mint leaves before serving.

Nutritional Information:

Calories: 35, Protein: 0g, Carbohydrates: 9g, Fat: 0g, Fiber: 1g, Cholesterol: 0mg, Sodium: 5mg, Potassium: 65mg

Moctails

CRANBERRY ORANGE COOLER

🍽 2 SERVINGS   ⏱ 10 MINUTES   🕐 0 MINUTES

Ingredients:

- 1 cup 100% cranberry juice
- 1 cup freshly squeezed orange juice
- 1/2 cup sparkling water
- 1 tablespoon lime juice
- 1 teaspoon honey (optional, for sweetness)
- Ice cubes
- Orange slices, for garnish
- Fresh cranberries, for garnish

Directions:

1. In a mixing pitcher, combine cranberry juice and freshly squeezed orange juice.
2. Add lime juice and a teaspoon of honey, stirring well to dissolve the honey.
3. Pour in the sparkling water and mix gently.
4. Fill two glasses with ice cubes and pour the cranberry orange mixture over the ice.
5. Garnish with orange slices and fresh cranberries.
6. Serve immediately and enjoy your low-calorie refresher.

Nutritional Information:

Calories: 65, Protein: 1g, Carbohydrates: 16g, Fat: 0g, Fiber: 2g, Cholesterol: 0mg, Sodium: 5mg, Potassium: 250mg

LOW-CAL CUCUMBER MINT REFRESHER

🍽 2 SERVINGS   ⏱ 10 MINUTES   🕐 0 MINUTES

Ingredients:

- 1 cup cucumber, peeled and chopped
- 10 fresh mint leaves
- 1 tablespoon lime juice
- 1 teaspoon honey (optional)
- 2 cups sparkling water
- Ice cubes

Directions:

1. Blend the chopped cucumber and mint leaves until smooth.
2. Strain the mixture through a strainer into a bowl or pitcher.
3. Stir in the lime juice and honey (if using) until well combined.
4. Divide the mixture between two glasses filled with ice cubes.
5. Top each glass with sparkling water and gently stir to combine.
6. Garnish with a mint sprig or cucumber slice if desired.
7. Serve immediately and enjoy the refreshing taste!

Nutritional Information:

Calories: 15, Protein: 0g, Carbohydrates: 4g, Fat: 0g, Fiber: 0g, Cholesterol: 0mg, Sodium: 10mg, Potassium: 60mg

BERRY LIGHT SPARKLER

🍽 2 SERVINGS   ⏱ 10 MINUTES   🕐 0 MINUTES

Ingredients:

- 1 cup fresh mixed berries (strawberries, blueberries, raspberries)
- 1 tablespoon fresh lemon juice
- 4 fresh mint leaves
- 1 teaspoon honey or agave syrup
- 1 cup sparkling water
- Ice cubes, as needed

Directions:

1. Blend the mixed berries and lemon juice until smooth.
2. Strain the berry mixture through a strainer into a pitcher to remove seeds and pulp.
3. Muddle the mint leaves gently in the pitcher to release their flavor.
4. Stir in the honey or agave syrup until dissolved.
5. Pour in the sparkling water and stir gently.
6. Fill glasses with ice cubes and pour the berry mixture over the ice.
7. Garnish with additional mint leaves and a few whole berries, if desired.

Nutritional Information:

Calories: 40, Protein: 0.5g, Carbohydrates: 10g, Fat: 0g, Fiber: 3g, Cholesterol: 0 mg, Sodium: 5 mg, Potassium: 85 mg

CITRUS CLOUD ELIXIR

🍽 2 SERVINGS   ⏱ 5 MINUTES   🕐 0 MINUTES

Ingredients:

- 1 cup Freshly Squeezed Orange Juice
- 1/2 cup Freshly Squeezed Lemon Juice
- 1/4 cup Coconut Water
- 1 tablespoon Agave Syrup (optional)
- 1/2 cup Crushed Ice
- 1 tablespoon Aquafaba (chickpea water, for froth)

Directions:

1. Combine orange juice, lemon juice, coconut water, and agave syrup in the blender.
2. Add the crushed ice and aquafaba to the blender.
3. Blend on high speed for about 30 seconds until smooth and frothy.
4. Pour the mixture into two glasses.
5. Serve immediately, garnished with a slice of citrus fruit, if desired.

Nutritional Information:

Calories: 80, Protein: 1g, Carbohydrates: 19g, Fat: 0g, Fiber: 1g, Cholesterol: 0 mg, Sodium: 40 mg, Potassium: 320 mg

Mocktails

WATERMELON MINT DELIGHT

🍽 2 SERVINGS   ⏱ 10 MINUTES   🕒 0 MINUTES

Ingredients:

- 2 cups fresh watermelon, cubed
- 1/2 cup fresh mint leaves
- 1 tablespoon lime juice
- 1 teaspoon honey (optional)
- 1 cup ice cubes
- 1/2 cup sparkling water

Directions:

1. Combine watermelon cubes, mint leaves, lime juice, and honey in a blender.
2. Blend on high until smooth.
3. Pour the mixture through a fine mesh sieve into a pitcher, pressing down to extract all the juice.
4. Add ice cubes and stir in the sparkling water.
5. Serve immediately in chilled glasses, garnished with a sprig of mint.

Nutritional Information:

Calories: 45, Protein: 1g, Carbohydrates: 12g, Fat: 0g, Fiber: 1g, Cholesterol: 0 mg, Sodium: 2 mg, Potassium: 170 mg

ALOE VERA LEMON COOLER

🍽 2 SERVINGS   ⏱ 10 MINUTES   🕒 0 MINUTES

Ingredients:

- 1 cup Aloe Vera Juice
- 1/2 cup Fresh Lemon Juice
- 1 tablespoon Honey (or agave syrup for a vegan alternative)
- 1 cup Cold Sparkling Water
- Ice Cubes
- Lemon Slices, for garnish
- Fresh Mint Leaves, for garnish

Directions:

1. Combine aloe vera juice, lemon juice, and honey in a blender and blend until well mixed.
2. Fill glasses with ice cubes and pour the aloe-lemon mixture over the ice.
3. Top each glass with cold sparkling water for an effervescent finish.
4. Garnish with lemon slices and fresh mint leaves for a zesty touch.
5. Serve immediately and enjoy the crisp, low-calorie refreshment.

Nutritional Information:

Calories: 50, Protein: 0g, Carbohydrates: 13g, Fat: 0g, Fiber: 0g, Cholesterol: 0mg, Sodium: 5mg, Potassium: 20mg

Moctails

GREEN TEA LIME SPARKLE

2 SERVINGS   **10 MINUTES**   **5 MINUTES**

Ingredients:

- 2 cups Green tea, brewed and cooled
- 1 Lime, juiced
- 1 tsp Honey
- 1/2 cup Sparkling water
- Ice cubes, as needed
- Lime slices, for garnish
- Mint leaves, for garnish

Directions:

1. Brew the green tea using the kettle and allow it to cool to room temperature.
2. In a teapot, mix the lime juice and honey until the honey dissolves completely.
3. Add the cooled green tea into the teapot and whisk gently to combine the flavors.
4. Fill each glass with a few ice cubes and divide the green tea mixture evenly between the glasses.
5. Top each glass with sparkling water for a refreshing fizz.
6. Garnish with lime slices and mint leaves before serving.

Nutritional Information:

Calories: 25, Protein: 0g, Carbohydrates: 6g, Fat: 0g, Fiber: 1g, Cholesterol: 0mg, Sodium: 10mg, Potassium: 35mg

---

HIBISCUS SLIM SIP

2 SERVINGS   **5 MINUTES**   **10 MINUTES**

Ingredients:

- 2 cups Water
- 3 tablespoons Dried Hibiscus Flowers
- 1 tablespoon Agave Syrup
- 1/2 teaspoon Fresh Lime Juice
- 1/4 cup Sparkling Water
- Ice Cubes
- Lime Slices (for garnish)

Directions:

1. In a small saucepan, bring the water to a boil.
2. Add the dried hibiscus flowers to the boiling water and remove from heat.
3. Let the mixture steep for 10 minutes, then strain into a pitcher to remove the flowers.
4. Stir in the agave syrup and fresh lime juice until well combined.
5. Add sparkling water to the pitcher and stir gently.
6. Fill glasses with ice cubes and pour the hibiscus mixture over them.
7. Garnish with lime slices and serve immediately.

Nutritional Information:

Calories: 30, Protein: 0g, Carbohydrates: 8g, Fat: 0g, Fiber: 0g, Cholesterol: 0mg, Sodium: 5mg, Potassium: 20mg

Moctails

GRAPEFRUIT BASIL BLISS

2 SERVINGS | 10 MINUTES | 0 MINUTES

Ingredients:

- 1 large grapefruit, juiced
- 1/4 cup fresh basil leaves
- 1 tablespoon honey or agave syrup
- 1 cup sparkling water
- Ice cubes
- Grapefruit slices, for garnish
- Basil sprigs, for garnish

Directions:

1. Muddle the fresh basil leaves in a cocktail shaker to release their aroma.
2. Add grapefruit juice and honey or agave syrup to the shaker, and stir well.
3. Fill the shaker with ice cubes and shake vigorously until well mixed.
4. Strain the mixture into two glasses filled with ice.
5. Top each glass with sparkling water and gently stir to combine.
6. Garnish with grapefruit slices and basil sprigs before serving.

Nutritional Information:

Calories: 70, Protein: 1g, Carbohydrates: 18g, Fat: 0g, Fiber: 2g, Cholesterol: 0 mg, Sodium: 10 mg, Potassium: 260 mg

SKINNY PEACHY PUNCH

2 SERVINGS | 10 MINUTES | 0 MINUTES

Ingredients:

- 1 cup fresh peaches, sliced
- 1 cup peach-flavored sparkling water
- 1/2 cup fresh orange juice
- 1 tbsp fresh lime juice
- 1 tsp honey (optional)

Directions:

1. In a blender, combine the fresh peaches and orange juice and blend until smooth.
2. Pour the blended mixture through a strainer into a pitcher to remove pulp.
3. Add the sparkling water and lime juice to the pitcher, stirring gently to combine.
4. Taste, and add honey for extra sweetness if desired.
5. Serve over ice in chilled glasses, and garnish with a peach slice or mint if you like.

Nutritional Information:

Calories: 65, Protein: 1g, Carbohydrates: 16g, Fat: 0g, Fiber: 2g, Cholesterol: 0 mg, Sodium: 5 mg, Potassium: 210 mg

Mocktails

Savory Sips

TOMATO BASIL COOLER

🍽 4 SERVINGS　　⏱ 10 MINUTES　　🕐 0 MINUTES

Ingredients:

- 4 cups ripe tomatoes, chopped
- 1 cup fresh basil leaves
- 1 tablespoon lemon juice
- 1 teaspoon honey
- 1/2 teaspoon sea salt
- 2 cups chilled sparkling water
- Ice cubes (as desired)

Directions:

1. Combine the chopped tomatoes, basil leaves, lemon juice, honey, and sea salt in a blender.
2. Blend until the mixture is smooth.
3. Strain the blended mixture through a fine mesh strainer into a pitcher to remove the pulp.
4. Stir in the sparkling water gently.
5. Fill glasses with ice cubes and pour the Tomato Basil Cooler over the ice.
6. Garnish with additional basil leaves if desired and serve immediately.

Nutritional Information:

Calories: 45, Protein: 2g, Carbohydrates: 10g, Fat: 0g, Fiber: 2g, Cholesterol: 0mg, Sodium: 150mg, Potassium: 400mg

CUCUMBER DILL REFRESHER

🍽 2 SERVINGS　　⏱ 10 MINUTES　　🕐 0 MINUTES

Ingredients:

- 1 cup cucumber, peeled and chopped
- 2 tablespoons fresh dill, chopped
- 1 tablespoon lime juice
- 1 tablespoon honey (or agave for a vegan option)
- 1 cup water
- Ice cubes as needed
- Thin cucumber slices and dill sprigs for garnish

Directions:

1. In a blender, combine chopped cucumber, dill, lime juice, and honey with water.
2. Blend until smooth and well combined.
3. Strain the mixture through a fine sieve into a mixing pitcher to remove pulp.
4. Fill two glasses with ice cubes.
5. Pour the strained mixture over the ice in each glass.
6. Garnish with cucumber slices and a sprig of dill.
7. Serve immediately with a smile and savor each sip.

Nutritional Information:

Calories: 45, Protein: 1g, Carbohydrates: 12g, Fat: 0g, Fiber: 1g, Cholesterol: 0mg, Sodium: 5mg, Potassium: 150mg

Moctails

SPICED CARROT GINGER SPARK

4 SERVINGS | **10 MINUTES** | **0 MINUTES**

Ingredients:

- 2 cups Fresh Carrot Juice
- 1 tablespoon Fresh Ginger, grated
- 1 tablespoon Lemon Juice
- 1 teaspoon Ground Cumin
- 1 teaspoon Honey (optional, for sweetness)
- Pinch of Sea Salt
- 2 cups Sparkling Water
- Ice Cubes
- Fresh Mint Leaves, for garnish

Directions:

1. Combine carrot juice, grated ginger, lemon juice, ground cumin, honey, and sea salt in a blender. Blend until smooth.
2. Strain the mixture through a fine mesh strainer into a mixing pitcher to remove any solids.
3. Add sparkling water to the strained mixture and stir gently to combine.
4. Fill four glasses with ice cubes and pour the mocktail evenly into each glass.
5. Garnish with fresh mint leaves and serve immediately for a refreshing touch.

Nutritional Information:

Calories: 45, Protein: 1g, Carbohydrates: 11g, Fat: 0g, Fiber: 2g, Cholesterol: 0mg, Sodium: 30mg, Potassium: 320mg

BLOODY MARY MOCKTAIL

2 SERVINGS | **10 MINUTES** | **0 MINUTES**

Ingredients:

- 1 ½ cups Tomato Juice
- 2 tbsp Lemon Juice
- 2 tsp Worcestershire Sauce
- 1 tsp Hot Sauce (adjust to taste)
- ¼ tsp Celery Salt
- ¼ tsp Ground Black Pepper
- 2 Celery Stalks, for garnish
- 2 Lemon Wedges, for garnish

Directions:

1. In a blender, combine tomato juice, lemon juice, Worcestershire sauce, hot sauce, celery salt, and ground black pepper.
2. Blend the mixture briefly to ensure all ingredients are well combined.
3. Pour the mixture into a mixing glass filled halfway with ice.
4. Stir gently with a stirring spoon to chill the mocktail without diluting too much.
5. Strain into two tall glasses and garnish each with a celery stalk and a lemon wedge.

Nutritional Information:

Calories: 50, Protein: 2g, Carbohydrates: 11g, Fat: 0g, Fiber: 2g, Cholesterol: 0mg, Sodium: 650mg, Potassium: 560mg

Moctails

AVOCADO CILANTRO SMOOTH SIP

2 SERVINGS   **10 MINUTES**   **0 MINUTES**

Ingredients:

- 1 ripe Avocado
- 1 cup Fresh Cilantro leaves
- 2 cups Cold Water
- 1 tablespoon Lime Juice
- ½ teaspoon Sea Salt
- ¼ teaspoon Black Pepper
- 1 pinch Red Pepper Flakes (optional for heat)

Directions:

1. Halve the avocado, remove the pit, and scoop the flesh into the blender.
2. Add cilantro, cold water, lime juice, sea salt, and black pepper to the blender.
3. Blend on high speed until smooth and creamy.
4. Taste and adjust seasoning, adding red pepper flakes for a spicy kick if desired.
5. Pour into glasses and serve immediately for maximum freshness.

Nutritional Information:

Calories: 160, Protein: 3g, Carbohydrates: 11g, Fat: 13g, Fiber: 7g, Cholesterol: 0mg, Sodium: 310mg, Potassium: 500mg

JALAPEÑO LIME ZEST

4 SERVINGS   **10 MINUTES**   **0 MINUTES**

Ingredients:

- 2 cups sparkling water
- 1 large jalapeño, sliced (remove seeds for less heat)
- 1/4 cup freshly squeezed lime juice
- 1 tablespoon honey
- Ice cubes, as needed
- Lime wedges, for garnish
- Jalapeño slices, for garnish

Directions:

1. In a blender, combine sliced jalapeño, freshly squeezed lime juice, and honey. Blend until smooth.
2. Optional: Strain the blended mixture through a fine mesh strainer into a pitcher to remove jalapeño bits for a smoother texture.
3. Fill each serving glass with ice cubes.
4. Pour the jalapeño-lime mixture evenly into each glass.
5. Top each glass with sparkling water, gently stirring to combine.
6. Garnish with lime wedges and jalapeño slices.
7. Serve immediately and enjoy the zingy, spicy delight!

Nutritional Information:

Calories: 35, Protein: 0g, Carbohydrates: 9g, Fat: 0g, Fiber: 0g, Cholesterol: 0 mg, Sodium: 2 mg, Potassium: 58 mg

Mocktails

BEETROOT LEMON SPRITZ

4 SERVINGS | **10 MINUTES** | **0 MINUTES**

Ingredients:

- 1 cup Beetroot juice
- 1/2 cup Fresh lemon juice
- 1 cup Sparkling water
- 2 tbsp Honey or agave syrup
- 1/4 tsp Himalayan pink salt
- Ice cubes
- Lemon slices and mint leaves for garnish

Directions:

1. In a blender, combine beetroot juice, lemon juice, honey, and Himalayan pink salt.
2. Blend until the mixture is smooth and well combined.
3. Strain the mixture into a jug to remove any solids.
4. Add sparkling water to the strained mixture and stir gently.
5. Fill glasses with ice cubes, pour the beetroot lemon mixture over the ice, and garnish with lemon slices and mint leaves.
6. Serve immediately and enjoy a refreshing Beetroot Lemon Spritz.

Nutritional Information:

Calories: 50, Protein: 1g, Carbohydrates: 13g, Fat: 0g, Fiber: 2g, Cholesterol: 0 mg, Sodium: 95 mg, Potassium: 200 mg

CELERY SALT & LEMON FIZZ

2 SERVINGS | **10 MINUTES** | **0 MINUTES**

Ingredients:

- 1 tablespoon celery salt
- 2 tablespoons lemon juice, freshly squeezed
- 1 tablespoon honey or agave syrup
- 1 cup soda water
- Ice cubes
- Lemon slices, for garnish
- Fresh celery stalks, for garnish

Directions:

1. Rim the edges of two tall glasses with celery salt by dipping them in water and then into the celery salt.
2. In a shaker, combine lemon juice and honey. Shake well until the honey is fully dissolved.
3. Fill glasses with ice cubes and strain the lemon mixture into them.
4. Top each glass with soda water, stirring gently to combine.
5. Garnish with a lemon slice and a fresh celery stalk before serving.

Nutritional Information:

Calories: 40, Protein: 0g, Carbohydrates: 11g, Fat: 0g, Fiber: 0g, Cholesterol: 0 mg, Sodium: 300 mg, Potassium: 60 mg

Moctails

TURMERIC TAMARIND TONIC

🍽 4 SERVINGS   ⏱ 10 MINUTES   ⏲ 0 MINUTES

Ingredients:

- 1 teaspoon turmeric powder
- 3 tablespoons tamarind paste
- 2 cups chilled coconut water
- 1 tablespoon lime juice
- 1 tablespoon honey
- Pinch of black pepper
- Ice cubes (for serving)

Directions:

1. In a blender, combine turmeric powder, tamarind paste, coconut water, lime juice, honey, and a pinch of black pepper.
2. Blend until all ingredients are well mixed and the mixture turns smooth.
3. Pour the blended mixture through a fine mesh strainer to remove any solids.
4. Taste and adjust sweetness or acidity by adding more honey or lime juice, if needed.
5. Serve over ice cubes, and garnish with a lime slice if desired.

Nutritional Information:

Calories: 60, Protein: 1g, Carbohydrates: 15g, Fat: 0g, Fiber: 2g, Cholesterol: 0 mg, Sodium: 15 mg, Potassium: 120 mg

SWEET POTATO MAPLE SWIRL

🍽 4 SERVINGS   ⏱ 10 MINUTES   ⏲ 20 MINUTES

Ingredients:

- 2 cups roasted sweet potato, mashed
- 3 cups water
- 1/4 cup pure maple syrup
- 1 teaspoon vanilla extract
- 1/2 teaspoon cinnamon
- 1/4 teaspoon nutmeg
- Pinch of salt
- Ice cubes (optional)

Directions:

1. Combine roasted sweet potato and water in a saucepan. Heat over medium, stirring occasionally, for about 5 minutes.
2. Add maple syrup, vanilla extract, cinnamon, nutmeg, and a pinch of salt, stirring until well mixed. Simmer for an additional 5 minutes.
3. Allow the mixture to cool slightly, then transfer to a blender. Blend until smooth and creamy.
4. Strain the mixture through a strainer to remove any solids, pressing with a spoon for maximum extraction.
5. Chill the mocktail or serve over ice cubes for a refreshing experience.

Nutritional Information:

Calories: 120, Protein: 1g, Carbohydrates: 29g, Fat: 0g, Fiber: 2g, Cholesterol: 0mg, Sodium: 40mg, Potassium: 220mg

Moctails

SMOKY PAPRIKA CITRUS SPLASH

2 SERVINGS   10 MINUTES   0 MINUTES

Ingredients:

- 1 cup fresh orange juice
- 1/2 cup fresh grapefruit juice
- 1/4 teaspoon smoked paprika
- 1 tablespoon honey
- 1/4 teaspoon sea salt
- Ice cubes, as needed
- 1 slice of orange (for garnish)
- 1 slice of grapefruit (for garnish)

Directions:

1. In a shaker, combine the fresh orange juice, grapefruit juice, smoked paprika, honey, and sea salt.
2. Fill the shaker with ice cubes, then secure the lid and shake vigorously for about 15 seconds.
3. Strain the mixture into two serving glasses filled with ice.
4. Garnish each glass with a slice of orange and grapefruit on the rim.
5. Serve immediately and enjoy the vibrant fusion of smoky and citrus flavors.

Nutritional Information:

Calories: 90, Protein: 1g, Carbohydrates: 22g, Fat: 0g, Fiber: 1g, Cholesterol: 0mg, Sodium: 155mg, Potassium: 325mg

PICKLED CUCUMBER COOLER

4 SERVINGS   10 MINUTES   0 MINUTES

Ingredients:

- 1 large cucumber, peeled and sliced
- 1/2 cup pickling liquid (from store-bought pickles)
- 1 tablespoon honey
- 2 tablespoons freshly squeezed lime juice
- 1 cup chilled sparkling water
- 1 tablespoon chopped fresh dill, plus extra for garnish
- Salt to taste
- Ice cubes

Directions:

1. Add cucumber slices to a blender and blend until smooth.
2. Strain the cucumber juice into a mixing pitcher to remove pulp.
3. Stir in the pickling liquid, honey, lime juice, and chopped dill into the cucumber juice.
4. Add salt to taste, ensuring the flavors are balanced to your preference.
5. Pour the mixture over ice cubes in glasses, leaving room to top with sparkling water.
6. Top each glass with chilled sparkling water and stir gently.
7. Garnish with a sprig of fresh dill and enjoy immediately.

Nutritional Information:

Calories: 28, Protein: 0g, Carbohydrates: 8g, Fat: 0g, Fiber: 0g, Cholesterol: 0mg, Sodium: 150mg, Potassium: 120mg

Moctails

Energizing Boosts

MATCHA MINT COOLER

2 SERVINGS | **10 MINUTES** | **0 MINUTES**

Ingredients:
- 2 tsp Matcha Powder
- 1 cup Coconut Water
- 1/2 cup Fresh Mint Leaves
- 1 tbsp Honey or Agave Syrup
- 1/2 Lime, juiced
- Ice Cubes
- Fresh Mint Sprigs, for garnish

Directions:
1. Blend matcha powder, coconut water, fresh mint leaves, honey, and lime juice until smooth.
2. Strain the mixture through a small sieve to remove mint leaf bits for a smoother texture.
3. Pour the strained liquid into glasses filled with ice cubes.
4. Garnish with fresh mint sprigs.
5. Serve immediately to enjoy the refreshing flavors.

Nutritional Information:
Calories: 60, Protein: 1g, Carbohydrates: 12g, Fat: 0g, Fiber: 1g, Cholesterol: 0mg, Sodium: 40mg, Potassium: 150mg

ESPRESSO ORANGE TWIST

2 SERVINGS | **10 MINUTES** | **0 MINUTES**

Ingredients:
- 1/2 cup freshly brewed espresso
- 1 cup fresh orange juice
- 1 tablespoon honey
- 1/2 teaspoon vanilla extract
- Ice cubes
- Orange slices for garnish

Directions:
1. Brew the espresso and let it cool slightly.
2. In a shaker, combine the orange juice, honey, and vanilla extract.
3. Add the cooled espresso into the shaker and fill with ice cubes.
4. Shake vigorously until well chilled.
5. Strain the mixture into two glasses filled with ice.
6. Garnish with orange slices and enjoy the refreshing boost!

Nutritional Information:
Calories: 85, Protein: 1g, Carbohydrates: 22g, Fat: 0g, Fiber: 1g, Cholesterol: 0mg, Sodium: 5mg, Potassium: 260mg

Moctails

BEET GINGER BOOSTER

🍽️ 2 SERVINGS ⏱️ 10 MINUTES 🕐 0 MINUTES

Ingredients:

- 1 medium beet, peeled and chopped
- 1 inch piece fresh ginger, peeled and chopped
- 1 cup fresh orange juice
- 1 tablespoon honey
- 1/2 cup chilled sparkling water
- Ice cubes

Directions:

1. Combine beet, ginger, and orange juice in a blender.
2. Blend until smooth, ensuring all ingredients are fully incorporated.
3. Strain the mixture through a fine mesh strainer or cheesecloth into a pitcher, removing any pulp.
4. Stir in honey until dissolved.
5. Pour mocktail into glasses over ice cubes, leaving some space for sparkling water.
6. Top with chilled sparkling water, gently stirring to mix.
7. Garnish with an orange slice or ginger slice if desired, then serve immediately.

Nutritional Information:

Calories: 78, Protein: 1g, Carbohydrates: 20g, Fat: 0g, Fiber: 2g, Cholesterol: 0 mg, Sodium: 25 mg, Potassium: 360 mg

COCONUT ESPRESSO SPARK

🍽️ 2 SERVINGS ⏱️ 5 MINUTES 🕐 0 MINUTES

Ingredients:

- 1 cup coconut milk
- 1/2 cup brewed espresso, cooled
- 1 tablespoon agave syrup or honey
- 1/4 teaspoon vanilla extract
- Ice cubes for serving
- Shredded coconut and cocoa powder for garnish (optional)

Directions:

1. Brew espresso and let it cool.
2. In a blender, combine coconut milk, cooled espresso, agave syrup, and vanilla extract.
3. Blend until smooth and frothy.
4. Fill two glasses with ice cubes and pour the coconut espresso mixture over the ice.
5. Garnish with a sprinkle of shredded coconut and cocoa powder if desired. Serve immediately.

Nutritional Information:

Calories: 125, Protein: 1g, Carbohydrates: 15g, Fat: 7g, Fiber: 1g, Cholesterol: 0 mg, Sodium: 45 mg, Potassium: 210 mg

Moctails

LEMON CHIA ENERGIZER

2 SERVINGS   **5 MINUTES**   **0 MINUTES**

Ingredients:

- 2 tablespoons chia seeds
- 1 cup cold water
- 1 cup fresh lemon juice
- 2 tablespoons honey (or agave syrup)
- 1/2 teaspoon grated ginger
- Ice cubes, as needed
- Lemon slices and mint leaves, for garnish

Directions:

1. In a pitcher, combine chia seeds and cold water. Stir well and let them soak for about 5 minutes until they swell.
2. Add fresh lemon juice, honey, and grated ginger to the soaked chia seeds. Mix thoroughly until the honey dissolves.
3. Fill glasses with ice cubes and pour the lemon chia mixture over the ice.
4. Garnish with lemon slices and mint leaves.
5. Stir gently before serving to ensure even distribution of chia seeds.

Nutritional Information:

Calories: 90, Protein: 2g, Carbohydrates: 23g, Fat: 1.5g, Fiber: 3g, Cholesterol: 0 mg, Sodium: 5 mg, Potassium: 60 mg

GREEN TEA CITRUS CHARGE

2 SERVINGS   **10 MINUTES**   **0 MINUTES**

Ingredients:

- 2 cups brewed green tea, cooled
- 1 tablespoon honey
- 1 tablespoon freshly squeezed lemon juice
- 1 tablespoon freshly squeezed orange juice
- 1/2 teaspoon grated ginger
- Lemon slices and mint leaves for garnish

Directions:

1. Whisk together the cooled green tea and honey in a mixing bowl until the honey dissolves.
2. Add the lemon juice, orange juice, and grated ginger to the bowl and mix well.
3. Pour the mixture into two glasses filled with ice.
4. Garnish each glass with lemon slices and mint leaves.
5. Serve immediately and enjoy the refreshing boost.

Nutritional Information:

Calories: 40, Protein: 0g, Carbohydrates: 10g, Fat: 0g, Fiber: 0g, Cholesterol: 0 mg, Sodium: 5 mg, Potassium: 20 mg

Moctails

GUARANA BERRY BLISS

2 SERVINGS   10 MINUTES   0 MINUTES

Ingredients:

- 1 cup mixed berries (strawberries, blueberries, raspberries)
- 1 teaspoon guarana powder
- 1 tablespoon honey or agave syrup
- 1 cup unsweetened coconut water
- ½ cup ice cubes
- ½ lime, juiced
- Fresh mint leaves for garnish

Directions:

1. Add mixed berries, guarana powder, honey, coconut water, ice cubes, and lime juice into a blender.
2. Blend the mixture until smooth and well-combined.
3. Strain the blend through a fine mesh strainer into a serving glass to remove seeds and pulp.
4. Stir gently and garnish with fresh mint leaves.
5. Serve immediately and enjoy the energizing boost.

Nutritional Information:

Calories: 100, Protein: 1g, Carbohydrates: 24g, Fat: 0g, Fiber: 3g, Cholesterol: 0mg, Sodium: 40mg, Potassium: 200mg

GINSENG GRAPEFRUIT FIZZ

2 SERVINGS   10 MINUTES   0 MINUTES

Ingredients:

- 1 teaspoon ginseng powder
- 1 cup fresh grapefruit juice
- 1/2 cup sparkling water
- 1 tablespoon honey (optional)
- Ice cubes
- Grapefruit slices, for garnish
- Mint leaves, for garnish

Directions:

1. In a cocktail shaker, combine ginseng powder, fresh grapefruit juice, and honey.
2. Add ice cubes to the shaker and shake vigorously for about 30 seconds.
3. Strain the mixture evenly into two glasses filled with ice cubes.
4. Top each glass with sparkling water and gently stir to combine.
5. Garnish with grapefruit slices and mint leaves before serving.

Nutritional Information:

Calories: 65, Protein: 0g, Carbohydrates: 17g, Fat: 0g, Fiber: 1g, Cholesterol: 0 mg, Sodium: 10 mg, Potassium: 170 mg

Moctails

MANGO PROTEIN PUNCH

2 SERVINGS   **10 MINUTES**   **0 MINUTES**

Ingredients:

- 1 cup ripe mango chunks (fresh or frozen)
- 1 scoop vanilla protein powder
- 1 cup coconut water
- 1/2 cup Greek yogurt
- 1 tablespoon honey
- 1/2 teaspoon fresh lime juice
- Ice cubes (optional)

Directions:

1. Combine mango chunks, protein powder, coconut water, Greek yogurt, honey, and lime juice in the blender.
2. Blend on high speed until smooth and creamy.
3. Add ice cubes if desired and blend again for a chilled effect.
4. Pour into glasses and garnish with a slice of lime or mango, if desired.
5. Serve immediately for maximum freshness and potency.

Nutritional Information:

Calories: 225, Protein: 15g, Carbohydrates: 36g, Fat: 4g, Fiber: 2g, Cholesterol: 5mg, Sodium: 60mg, Potassium: 450mg

ACAI BERRY REFRESHER

2 SERVINGS   **10 MINUTES**   **0 MINUTES**

Ingredients:

- 1 cup Acai Juice
- 1/2 cup Coconut Water
- 1/2 cup Mixed Berries (fresh or frozen)
- 1 tablespoon Lime Juice
- 1 teaspoon Honey (optional for extra sweetness)
- Ice cubes, as desired

Directions:

1. Combine acai juice, coconut water, mixed berries, and lime juice in a blender.
2. Blend until smooth, ensuring all berries are well incorporated.
3. Taste and add honey if additional sweetness is desired.
4. Add ice cubes to serving glasses.
5. Pour the blended mixture over the ice.
6. Stir gently and garnish with a few whole berries, if desired.
7. Serve immediately and enjoy the energizing refreshment.

Nutritional Information:

Calories: 120, Protein: 1g, Carbohydrates: 30g, Fat: 0.5g, Fiber: 5g, Cholesterol: 0 mg, Sodium: 25 mg, Potassium: 150 mg

Moctails

PINEAPPLE SPIRULINA ZEST

🍽 2 SERVINGS   ⏱ 10 MINUTES   🕐 0 MINUTES

Ingredients:

- 1 cup Fresh Pineapple Chunks
- 1 ½ cups Coconut Water
- ½ teaspoon Spirulina Powder
- 1 tablespoon Lime Juice
- 1 teaspoon Honey or Agave Syrup (optional)
- Ice Cubes (as needed)
- Mint Leaves for Garnish (optional)

Directions:

1. Add the pineapple chunks, coconut water, spirulina powder, lime juice, and honey into the blender.
2. Blend until smooth and frothy.
3. Add ice cubes and blend again until the desired consistency is achieved.
4. Pour the mocktail into glasses and garnish with fresh mint leaves, if desired.
5. Serve immediately and enjoy the refreshing boost!

Nutritional Information:

Calories: 90, Protein: 1g, Carbohydrates: 21g, Fat: 0g, Fiber: 2g, Cholesterol: 0mg, Sodium: 15mg, Potassium: 200mg

TURMERIC HONEY GLOW

🍽 2 SERVINGS   ⏱ 10 MINUTES   🕐 0 MINUTES

Ingredients:

- 1 cup coconut water
- 1/2 teaspoon turmeric powder
- 1 tablespoon honey
- 1 tablespoon fresh lime juice
- 1/8 teaspoon ground ginger
- Ice cubes
- Lime slices and mint leaves, for garnish

Directions:

1. In a shaker, combine coconut water, turmeric, honey, lime juice, and ginger.
2. Add a handful of ice cubes to the shaker and shake vigorously for about 20 seconds.
3. Strain the mixture into two glasses filled with ice.
4. Garnish each glass with lime slices and fresh mint leaves.
5. Serve immediately and enjoy the refreshing glow.

Nutritional Information:

Calories: 80, Protein: 1g, Carbohydrates: 22g, Fat: 0g, Fiber: 1g, Cholesterol: 0mg, Sodium: 40mg, Potassium: 200mg

Moctails

Timeless Classics

VIRGIN MOJITO

🍽 2 SERVINGS   ⏱ 10 MINUTES   🕐 0 MINUTES

Ingredients:

- 10 fresh mint leaves
- 1 lime, cut into wedges
- 2 tablespoons sugar
- 1 cup club soda
- Ice cubes, as needed
- Mint sprigs, for garnish

Directions:

1. Place mint leaves and lime wedges in a shaker; muddle gently to release the lime juice and mint oils.
2. Add sugar, muddling again to combine and dissolve the sugar with the lime mixture.
3. Fill the shaker with ice cubes and pour in the club soda.
4. Shake well until the mixture is chilled and well combined.
5. Strain the mixture into two tall glasses filled with ice cubes.
6. Garnish with mint sprigs and serve immediately.

Nutritional Information:

Calories: 40, Protein: 0g, Carbohydrates: 11g, Fat: 0g, Fiber: 1g, Cholesterol: 0 mg, Sodium: 5 mg, Potassium: 20 mg

NON-ALCOHOLIC PIÑA COLADA

🍽 2 SERVINGS   ⏱ 5 MINUTES   🕐 0 MINUTES

Ingredients:

- 1 cup Pineapple Juice
- 1 cup Coconut Milk
- 1/2 cup Crushed Ice
- 2 tablespoons Sugar or Honey (optional)
- Pineapple Slices and Cherries (for garnish)

Directions:

1. Combine pineapple juice, coconut milk, crushed ice, and sugar (if using) in a blender.
2. Blend on high until smooth and creamy.
3. Taste and adjust sweetness if desired.
4. Pour into glasses and garnish with pineapple slices and cherries.
5. Serve immediately and enjoy your tropical escape.

Nutritional Information:

Calories: 180, Protein: 1g, Carbohydrates: 30g, Fat: 7g, Fiber: 2g, Cholesterol: 0 mg, Sodium: 20 mg, Potassium: 200 mg

Mocktails

CLASSIC SHIRLEY TEMPLE

🍽 2 SERVINGS   ⏱ 5 MINUTES   🕐 0 MINUTES

Ingredients:
- 6 oz Ginger Ale
- 6 oz Lemon-Lime Soda
- 1 oz Grenadine
- Maraschino Cherries, for garnish
- Orange Slice, for garnish

Directions:
1. Fill two highball glasses with ice cubes.
2. Pour 3 oz of ginger ale and 3 oz of lemon-lime soda into each glass.
3. Add 0.5 oz of grenadine to each glass, allow it to gently cascade through the drink.
4. Stir gently to combine, using a stirring stick.
5. Garnish with a maraschino cherry and a slice of orange on the rim of each glass.
6. Serve immediately with a smile.

Nutritional Information:
Calories: 120, Protein: 0g, Carbohydrates: 30g, Fat: 0g, Fiber: 0g, Cholesterol: 0mg, Sodium: 25mg, Potassium: 30mg

---

FAUX SANGRIA SPARKLE

🍽 4 SERVINGS   ⏱ 10 MINUTES   🕐 0 MINUTES

Ingredients:
- 2 cups pomegranate juice
- 1 cup orange juice
- 1 cup sparkling water or club soda
- 1/2 cup mixed fresh berries (e.g., strawberries, raspberries, blueberries)
- 1 orange, sliced
- 1 lemon, sliced
- 1/2 apple, sliced thinly
- Ice cubes

Directions:
1. In a large pitcher, combine the pomegranate juice and orange juice. Stir well to mix.
2. Add the mixed fresh berries, orange slices, lemon slices, and apple slices to the juice mixture.
3. Let the mixture chill in the refrigerator for at least 5 minutes to allow the flavors to meld.
4. Just before serving, add sparkling water to the pitcher and gently stir to combine.
5. Fill serving glasses with ice cubes and pour the faux sangria mixture over the ice.
6. Garnish with an extra slice of orange or a few fresh berries, if desired.

Nutritional Information:
Calories: 90, Protein: 1g, Carbohydrates: 23g, Fat: 0g, Fiber: 2g, Cholesterol: 0mg, Sodium: 5mg, Potassium: 230mg

Moctails

VIRGIN MARY

2 SERVINGS   5 MINUTES   0 MINUTES

Ingredients:

- 1 1/2 cups Tomato Juice
- 1 tablespoon Lemon Juice
- 1 teaspoon Worcestershire Sauce
- 1/2 teaspoon Hot Sauce (adjust to taste)
- 1/4 teaspoon Horseradish
- Pinch of Celery Salt
- Pinch of Ground Black Pepper
- Celery Stalk and Lemon Wedge for garnish

Directions:

1. In a shaker, combine tomato juice, lemon juice, Worcestershire sauce, hot sauce, horseradish, celery salt, and black pepper.
2. Shake well to mix all ingredients thoroughly.
3. Strain the mixture into two tall glasses filled with ice.
4. Garnish with a celery stalk and a lemon wedge.
5. Serve immediately and enjoy the refreshing flavors.

Nutritional Information:

Calories: 40, Protein: 2g, Carbohydrates: 10g, Fat: 0g, Fiber: 2g, Cholesterol: 0mg, Sodium: 640mg, Potassium: 450mg

NOJITO (ALCOHOL-FREE MOJITO)

2 SERVINGS   10 MINUTES   0 MINUTES

Ingredients:

- 10 Fresh Mint Leaves
- 1 tbsp Sugar
- 3 tbsp Fresh Lime Juice
- 1 cup Club Soda
- 1/2 cup Crushed Ice
- Lime Slices and Mint Sprigs (for garnish)

Directions:

1. Place the mint leaves and sugar into a cocktail shaker. Use a muddler to gently crush the mint leaves to release their aroma.
2. Add the lime juice into the shaker and stir until the sugar dissolves.
3. Fill the shaker with crushed ice, then pour in the club soda. Secure the lid and shake gently to mix.
4. Pour the mixture into tall glasses and garnish with lime slices and a sprig of mint.
5. Serve immediately, savoring the refreshing burst of mint and lime.

Nutritional Information:

Calories: 34, Protein: 0g, Carbohydrates: 9g, Fat: 0g, Fiber: 1g, Cholesterol: 0mg, Sodium: 15mg, Potassium: 40mg

Moctails

CLASSIC LEMON SPRITZER

 4 SERVINGS   10 MINUTES   0 MINUTES

Ingredients:

- 1 cup Fresh Lemon Juice (about 4-5 lemons)
- 3 cups Sparkling Water
- 1/4 cup Simple Syrup (adjust to taste)
- Ice Cubes
- Lemon Slices (for garnish)
- Fresh Mint Leaves (optional, for garnish)

Directions:

1. Use the citrus juicer to extract lemon juice into the pitcher.
2. Add sparkling water and simple syrup to the pitcher, stirring gently with a large spoon until combined.
3. Fill each serving glass with ice cubes.
4. Pour the lemon mixture over the ice, filling each glass.
5. Garnish with lemon slices and fresh mint leaves, if desired.
6. Serve immediately and enjoy the refreshing taste!

Nutritional Information:

Calories: 45, Protein: 0g, Carbohydrates: 12g, Fat: 0g, Fiber: 0g, Cholesterol: 0mg, Sodium: 5mg, Potassium: 50mg

NON-ALCOHOLIC MARGARITA

 2 SERVINGS   10 MINUTES   0 MINUTES

Ingredients:

- 1 cup Fresh Lime Juice
- 1/2 cup Orange Juice
- 1/4 cup Agave Syrup or Simple Syrup
- 1 cup Sparkling Water
- Lime Wedges (for garnish)
- Salt (for rimming the glass)

Directions:

1. Rim the edge of each serving glass with lime juice and then dip in salt to coat.
2. In a blender, combine the lime juice, orange juice, and agave syrup. Blend until smooth.
3. Fill each glass with ice and pour the juice mixture over the ice.
4. Top with sparkling water, stirring gently to combine.
5. Garnish with lime wedges and serve immediately.

Nutritional Information:

Calories: 70, Protein: 0g, Carbohydrates: 18g, Fat: 0g, Fiber: 1g, Cholesterol: 0 mg, Sodium: 480 mg, Potassium: 60 mg

Moctails

ALCOHOL-FREE COSMO COOLER

2 SERVINGS **5 MINUTES** **0 MINUTES**

Ingredients:

- 1 cup Cranberry Juice
- 1/2 cup Fresh Orange Juice
- 1/4 cup Lime Juice
- 1/4 cup Sparkling Water
- 1 tablespoon Simple Syrup
- Lime Slices, for garnish
- Orange Peel, for garnish

Directions:

1. In a shaker, combine cranberry juice, fresh orange juice, lime juice, and simple syrup.
2. Fill the shaker with ice and shake vigorously until well chilled.
3. Strain the mixture into two cocktail glasses.
4. Top each glass with sparkling water.
5. Garnish with lime slices and a twist of orange peel.

Nutritional Information:

Calories: 95, Protein: 1g, Carbohydrates: 23g, Fat: 0g, Fiber: 1g, Cholesterol: 0mg, Sodium: 10mg, Potassium: 150mg

MIMOSA MOCKTAIL

2 SERVINGS **5 MINUTES** **0 MINUTES**

Ingredients:

- 1 cup Fresh Orange Juice
- 1 cup Chilled Sparkling Water
- 1 tablespoon Lemon Juice
- Orange Slices, for garnish
- Mint Leaves, for garnish (optional)

Directions:

1. Juice fresh oranges to obtain 1 cup of orange juice.
2. Combine the orange juice and lemon juice in a mixing jug.
3. Slowly add chilled sparkling water to the juice mixture, stirring gently.
4. Pour the mixture into two serving glasses.
5. Garnish each glass with an orange slice and optional mint leaves for a fresh look.

Nutritional Information:

Calories: 45, Protein: 1g, Carbohydrates: 11g, Fat: 0g, Fiber: 1g, Cholesterol: 0mg, Sodium: 5mg, Potassium: 200mg

Mocktails

APPLE CIDER SPRITZ

2 SERVINGS   5 MINUTES   0 MINUTES

Ingredients:

- 1 cup Chilled Sparkling Apple Cider
- 1/2 cup Club Soda
- 1/4 cup Cranberry Juice
- 1/2 tsp Lemon Juice
- Optional: Apple Slices and Fresh Cranberries for Garnish

Directions:

1. In a mixing glass, combine chilled sparkling apple cider and club soda.
2. Add cranberry juice and lemon juice to the mixture, stirring gently.
3. Pour the mocktail evenly into two glasses filled with ice.
4. Garnish with apple slices and fresh cranberries if desired.
5. Serve immediately and enjoy the refreshing taste.

Nutritional Information:

Calories: 80, Protein: 0g, Carbohydrates: 20g, Fat: 0g, Fiber: 1g, Cholesterol: 0 mg, Sodium: 10 mg, Potassium: 90 mg

NON-ALCOHOLIC MARTINI TWIST

2 SERVINGS   5 MINUTES   0 MINUTES

Ingredients:

- 1 cup Chilled White Grape Juice
- 1/4 cup Freshly Squeezed Lemon Juice
- 2 teaspoons Olive Brine
- 2 drops Non-Alcoholic Bitters
- Ice Cubes (as needed)
- Lemon Peel Twist (for garnish)

Directions:

1. Fill the shaker halfway with ice cubes.
2. Pour in the chilled white grape juice, lemon juice, olive brine, and bitters.
3. Shake vigorously for about 20 seconds until well chilled.
4. Strain the mixture into chilled martini glasses, discarding the ice.
5. Garnish with a twist of lemon peel. Serve immediately.

Nutritional Information:

Calories: 90, Protein: 0.3g, Carbohydrates: 24g, Fat: 0.2g, Fiber: 0.5g, Cholesterol: 0 mg, Sodium: 250 mg, Potassium: 250 mg

Dessert-Inspired Drinks

CHOCOLATE MINT BLISS

2 SERVINGS   10 MINUTES   0 MINUTES

Ingredients:

- 2 cups Milk (dairy or non-dairy)
- 2 tablespoons Cocoa Powder
- 2 tablespoons Chocolate Syrup
- 1 tablespoon Honey or Sweetener of choice
- 1 teaspoon Peppermint Extract
- Ice Cubes (as needed)
- Fresh Mint Leaves (for garnish)
- Crushed Chocolate (for rim garnish, optional)

Directions:

1. Prepare the Blender: Add milk, cocoa powder, chocolate syrup, and honey into the blender.
2. Blend: Add peppermint extract and a handful of ice cubes. Blend until smooth and frothy.
3. Rim the Glasses: If desired, lightly crush some chocolate and rim the glasses with it.
4. Pour and Garnish: Pour the mix into chilled glasses. Garnish with fresh mint leaves.
5. Serve: Serve immediately to enjoy the cool, refreshing blend of chocolate and mint.

Nutritional Information:

Calories: 210, Protein: 6g, Carbohydrates: 31g, Fat: 8g, Fiber: 2g, Cholesterol: 10mg, Sodium: 100mg, Potassium: 320mg

VANILLA BEAN CREAM SODA

4 SERVINGS   10 MINUTES   0 MINUTES

Ingredients:

- 4 cups soda water
- 1 cup heavy cream
- 2 tablespoons vanilla bean syrup
- 2 tablespoons granulated sugar
- Ice cubes

Directions:

1. In a pitcher, combine soda water and vanilla bean syrup. Stir gently to mix.
2. Add heavy cream and granulated sugar to the mixture. Stir until the sugar is dissolved.
3. Fill each glass with ice cubes.
4. Pour the vanilla cream soda mixture over the ice in each glass.
5. Stir gently before serving to maintain the creaminess.

Nutritional Information:

Calories: 120, Protein: 1g, Carbohydrates: 15g, Fat: 8g, Fiber: 0g, Cholesterol: 25mg, Sodium: 15mg, Potassium: 40mg

Mocktails

STRAWBERRY CHEESECAKE SHAKE

🍽 2 SERVINGS ⏱ 10 MINUTES 🕐 0 MINUTES

Ingredients:

- 1 cup Fresh Strawberries, hulled and sliced
- 1 cup Vanilla Greek Yogurt
- 1/2 cup Milk (or non-dairy alternative)
- 2 tablespoons Cream Cheese, softened
- 1 tablespoon Honey
- 1/2 teaspoon Vanilla Extract
- 1/2 cup Ice Cubes
- Optional: Crushed Graham Crackers for garnish

Directions:

1. Place sliced strawberries, Greek yogurt, milk, softened cream cheese, honey, and vanilla extract into the blender.
2. Add the ice cubes to the mixture.
3. Blend on high until the ingredients are smooth and creamy.
4. Pour the shake into two glasses.
5. Optionally, top with crushed graham crackers for a cheesecake-like texture.
6. Serve immediately for best flavor.

Nutritional Information:

Calories: 210, Protein: 8g, Carbohydrates: 30g, Fat: 7g, Fiber: 2g, Cholesterol: 15mg, Sodium: 100mg, Potassium: 360mg

KEY LIME PIE REFRESHER

🍽 2 SERVINGS ⏱ 10 MINUTES 🕐 0 MINUTES

Ingredients:

- 1/2 cup Key Lime Juice (freshly squeezed)
- 1/4 cup Coconut Cream
- 1 tablespoon Agave Syrup
- 1/2 cup Graham Cracker Crumbs
- 1 cup Crushed Ice
- 1/4 teaspoon Vanilla Extract
- Lime Slices (for garnish)
- Whipped Cream (for garnish, optional)

Directions:

1. In a blender, combine the key lime juice, coconut cream, agave syrup, and vanilla extract.
2. Add the crushed ice and blend on high until smooth and frothy.
3. Rim the serving glasses with graham cracker crumbs by dipping them in water and then into the crumbs.
4. Pour the blended mixture into the prepared glasses.
5. Garnish with a lime slice on the rim and add a dollop of whipped cream if desired.

Nutritional Information:

Calories: 150, Protein: 1g, Carbohydrates: 23g, Fat: 8g, Fiber: 1g, Cholesterol: 0mg, Sodium: 35mg, Potassium: 150mg

Moctails

SALTED CARAMEL SPRITZ

2 SERVINGS **10 MINUTES** **0 MINUTES**

Ingredients:

- 2 tbsp Salted Caramel Syrup
- 1 cup Sparkling Water
- 1/2 cup Fresh Apple Juice
- 1 tbsp Fresh Lemon Juice
- Pinch Sea Salt
- Crushed Ice
- Caramel Sauce (for garnish)
- Sea Salt Flakes (for garnish)

Directions:

1. Drizzle caramel sauce around the rim of each glass and sprinkle lightly with sea salt flakes.
2. In a shaker, combine salted caramel syrup, fresh apple juice, fresh lemon juice, and a pinch of sea salt.
3. Fill the shaker with crushed ice and shake vigorously to combine.
4. Strain the mixture evenly into two prepared glasses filled with additional crushed ice.
5. Top with sparkling water, stirring gently to mix.
6. Garnish with a thin apple slice or a twist of lemon peel, if desired, and serve chilled.

Nutritional Information:

Calories: 70, Protein: 0g, Carbohydrates: 18g, Fat: 0g, Fiber: 0g, Cholesterol: 0mg, Sodium: 55mg, Potassium: 15mg

---

BANOFFEE CREAM COOLER

2 SERVINGS **10 MINUTES** **0 MINUTES**

Ingredients:

- 1 ripe banana
- 1 cup milk (dairy or plant-based)
- 1/4 cup caramel sauce
- 1/4 teaspoon vanilla extract
- 1/4 cup whipped cream (for topping)
- 2 tablespoons crushed graham crackers (for garnish)
- Ice cubes

Directions:

1. Peel the banana and cut it into chunks. Add to the blender.
2. Pour in the milk, caramel sauce, and vanilla extract.
3. Add a handful of ice cubes to the blender to create a chilled drink.
4. Blend the mixture until smooth and creamy.
5. Pour the mocktail into glasses, then top with whipped cream.
6. Garnish each drink with a sprinkle of crushed graham crackers. Serve immediately.

Nutritional Information:

Calories: 250, Protein: 5g, Carbohydrates: 40g, Fat: 8g, Fiber: 2g, Cholesterol: 15mg, Sodium: 120mg, Potassium: 400mg

Mocktails

CINNAMON ROLL ELIXIR

🍽️ 2 SERVINGS   ⏱️ 10 MINUTES   🕐 0 MINUTES

Ingredients:

- 1 cup almond milk
- 1/2 cup unsweetened coconut milk
- 2 tablespoons maple syrup
- 1 teaspoon vanilla extract
- 1 teaspoon ground cinnamon
- 1/4 teaspoon ground nutmeg
- Ice cubes (optional, for a chilled drink)

Directions:

1. In a blender, combine the almond milk and coconut milk until well mixed.
2. Add the maple syrup, vanilla extract, ground cinnamon, and ground nutmeg to the blender.
3. Blend the mixture on medium speed for 30 seconds or until ingredients are well incorporated.
4. If you prefer a chilled drink, add a handful of ice cubes to the blender and blend again until smooth.
5. Pour the Cinnamon Roll Elixir into two glasses and garnish with a light sprinkle of cinnamon on top.

Nutritional Information:

Calories: 130, Protein: 2g, Carbohydrates: 18g, Fat: 5g, Fiber: 1g, Cholesterol: 0 mg, Sodium: 120 mg, Potassium: 180 mg

TIRAMISU MOCKTAIL

🍽️ 2 SERVINGS   ⏱️ 10 MINUTES   🕐 0 MINUTES

Ingredients:

- 1 cup Cold Brew Coffee
- 1 cup Almond Milk
- 2 tablespoons Mascarpone Cheese
- 2 tablespoons Chocolate Syrup
- 1 tablespoon Sugar
- 1/2 teaspoon Vanilla Extract
- Ice Cubes
- Cocoa Powder for Garnish

Directions:

1. Blend the cold brew coffee, almond milk, mascarpone cheese, chocolate syrup, sugar, and vanilla extract until smooth.
2. Fill glasses with ice cubes.
3. Pour the blended mixture over the ice.
4. Stir gently with a long spoon to combine.
5. Garnish with a light dusting of cocoa powder.

Nutritional Information:

Calories: 150, Protein: 3g, Carbohydrates: 22g, Fat: 5g, Fiber: 1g, Cholesterol: 10mg, Sodium: 90mg, Potassium: 300mg

Moctails

ALMOND JOY REFRESHER

2 SERVINGS   10 MINUTES   0 MINUTES

Ingredients:

- 1 cup coconut milk
- 2 tablespoons almond syrup
- 1 cup ice cubes
- 2 teaspoons unsweetened cocoa powder
- 1 tablespoon shredded coconut
- 2 tablespoons chocolate syrup (for garnish)
- 2 tablespoons sliced almonds (for garnish)

Directions:

1. Pour coconut milk, almond syrup, ice cubes, and cocoa powder into a blender.
2. Blend on high until smooth and creamy.
3. Rim the serving glasses with chocolate syrup.
4. Pour the blended mixture into the prepared glasses.
5. Garnish with shredded coconut and sliced almonds on top.
6. Serve immediately and enjoy the dessert-inspired refreshment.

Nutritional Information:

Calories: 220, Protein: 2g, Carbohydrates: 27g, Fat: 12g, Fiber: 3g, Cholesterol: 0mg, Sodium: 35mg, Potassium: 180mg

RASPBERRY CHOCOLATE BLISS

2 SERVINGS   10 MINUTES   0 MINUTES

Ingredients:

- 1 cup raspberries
- 1 1/2 cups almond milk
- 2 tbsp cocoa powder
- 2 tbsp honey or agave syrup
- 1/2 tsp vanilla extract
- Ice cubes
- Optional garnish: whipped cream, chocolate shavings, or extra raspberries

Directions:

1. In a blender, combine raspberries, almond milk, cocoa powder, honey, and vanilla extract. Blend until smooth.
2. Strain the mixture through a fine mesh sieve into a shaker to remove raspberry seeds.
3. Add ice cubes to the shaker and shake vigorously until well chilled.
4. Pour the mixture into two serving glasses.
5. If desired, top with whipped cream and garnish with chocolate shavings or extra raspberries.

Nutritional Information:

Calories: 160, Protein: 3g, Carbohydrates: 28g, Fat: 5g, Fiber: 6g, Cholesterol: 0mg, Sodium: 85mg, Potassium: 370mg

Moctails

S'MORES SHAKE FIZZ

🍽 2 SERVINGS   ⏱ 10 MINUTES   🕐 0 MINUTES

Ingredients:

- 1 cup milk (dairy or plant-based)
- 4 tablespoons chocolate syrup
- 1 tablespoon graham cracker crumbs
- 1 teaspoon vanilla extract
- 1/4 cup marshmallow fluff
- 1 cup club soda
- Ice cubes

Directions:

1. In a blender, combine milk, chocolate syrup, graham cracker crumbs, vanilla extract, and marshmallow fluff. Blend until smooth.
2. Pour the mixture into a shaker filled with ice cubes.
3. Shake the mixture vigorously for 30 seconds until chilled.
4. Fill each serving glass halfway with the chocolate-milk mixture.
5. Top with club soda, stirring gently to combine.
6. Garnish with a sprinkle of graham cracker crumbs and a dollop of marshmallow fluff on top.
7. Serve immediately with a straw and enjoy the fizzy, s'mores-infused delight.

Nutritional Information:

Calories: 160, Protein: 4g, Carbohydrates: 30g, Fat: 3g, Fiber: 1g, Cholesterol: 5mg, Sodium: 80mg, Potassium: 140mg

COCONUT CREAM DELIGHT

🍽 2 SERVINGS   ⏱ 10 MINUTES   🕐 0 MINUTES

Ingredients:

- 1 cup coconut milk
- 1/2 cup pineapple juice
- 1/4 cup cream of coconut
- 1 tablespoon vanilla syrup
- 1 cup ice cubes
- 2 tablespoons whipped cream (optional for garnish)
- 2 tablespoons toasted coconut flakes (optional for garnish)

Directions:

1. In a blender, combine coconut milk, pineapple juice, cream of coconut, vanilla syrup, and ice cubes.
2. Blend on high speed until the mixture is smooth and creamy.
3. Taste and adjust sweetness with additional vanilla syrup if desired.
4. Pour the mocktail into two glasses.
5. Top with whipped cream and sprinkle with toasted coconut flakes if using.

Nutritional Information:

Calories: 180, Protein: 1g, Carbohydrates: 19g, Fat: 13g, Fiber: 2g, Cholesterol: 5mg, Sodium: 25mg, Potassium: 200mg

Mocktails

Herbal Infusions

LAVENDER LEMONADE COOLER

4 SERVINGS | **10 MINUTES** | **5 MINUTES**

Ingredients:

- 2 cups water
- 1 tablespoon dried culinary lavender
- 1/2 cup freshly squeezed lemon juice
- 1/4 cup honey or agave syrup
- 2 cups cold sparkling water
- Ice cubes
- Lemon slices and lavender sprigs for garnish

Directions:

1. In a saucepan, bring 2 cups of water to a boil, then remove from heat.
2. Add dried lavender to the hot water, cover, and steep for 5 minutes.
3. Strain the lavender infusion into a pitcher, discarding the lavender flowers.
4. Stir in the lemon juice and honey until well combined.
5. Add the cold sparkling water to the mixture and stir gently.
6. Serve over ice in glasses, garnishing with lemon slices and lavender sprigs.

Nutritional Information:

Calories: 55, Protein: 0g, Carbohydrates: 14g, Fat: 0g, Fiber: 0g, Cholesterol: 0mg, Sodium: 5mg, Potassium: 25mg

---

ROSEMARY CITRUS SPARKLER

4 SERVINGS | **10 MINUTES** | **5 MINUTES**

Ingredients:

- 2 cups fresh grapefruit juice
- 1 cup sparkling water
- 2 tablespoons honey
- 2 sprigs fresh rosemary
- 1 teaspoon lemon zest
- Ice cubes
- Grapefruit slices (for garnish)

Directions:

1. In a saucepan, gently heat honey and rosemary sprigs over low heat for 3 minutes to infuse flavors.
2. Remove from heat and allow the rosemary-honey mixture to cool.
3. In a pitcher, combine the grapefruit juice, sparkling water, and cooled rosemary-infused honey. Stir well.
4. Add in the lemon zest and stir to combine all ingredients thoroughly.
5. Strain the mixture into glasses filled with ice cubes.
6. Garnish each glass with a grapefruit slice and an extra rosemary sprig, if desired.

Nutritional Information:

Calories: 65, Protein: 0g, Carbohydrates: 17g, Fat: 0g, Fiber: 1g, Cholesterol: 0mg, Sodium: 10mg, Potassium: 160mg

Mocktails

MINT & HONEY ELIXIR

2 SERVINGS   **10 MINUTES**   **5 MINUTES**

Ingredients:

- 1/2 cup fresh mint leaves
- 2 tablespoons honey
- 2 cups water
- 1 tablespoon lemon juice
- Ice cubes (optional)

Directions:

1. In a saucepan, bring the water to a gentle simmer.
2. Add mint leaves to the simmering water, and let it steep for 5 minutes.
3. Strain the mint-infused water into a jug and discard the leaves.
4. Stir in honey until fully dissolved, then add lemon juice.
5. Pour into glasses over ice cubes and garnish with additional mint leaves, if desired.

Nutritional Information:

Calories: 45, Protein: 0g,
Carbohydrates: 12g, Fat: 0g, Fiber: 0g,
Cholesterol: 0 mg, Sodium: 5 mg,
Potassium: 50 mg

BASIL BERRY BLISS

2 SERVINGS   **10 MINUTES**   **0 MINUTES**

Ingredients:

- 1 cup fresh mixed berries (strawberries, raspberries, blueberries)
- 10 fresh basil leaves
- 1 tablespoon honey or agave syrup
- 1 cup sparkling water
- 1/2 lemon, juiced
- Ice cubes
- Basil sprigs, for garnish

Directions:

1. Place mixed berries, basil leaves, honey, and lemon juice in the blender.
2. Blend until smooth, ensuring that basil is finely processed.
3. Strain the mixture into a pitcher using a strainer to remove seeds and pulp.
4. Add sparkling water to the strained juice and stir gently.
5. Fill two glasses with ice cubes and pour the basil berry mix over the ice.
6. Garnish each glass with a basil sprig and a few whole berries.
7. Serve immediately and enjoy the refreshing taste of Basil Berry Bliss.

Nutritional Information:

Calories: 60, Protein: 1g,
Carbohydrates: 16g, Fat: 0g, Fiber: 4g,
Cholesterol: 0mg, Sodium: 5mg,
Potassium: 120mg

CHAMOMILE CITRUS DREAM

🍽 2 SERVINGS ⏱ 10 MINUTES 🕐 5 MINUTES

Ingredients:

- 2 cups water
- 2 chamomile tea bags
- 1 cup freshly squeezed orange juice
- 1 tablespoon lemon juice
- 1 tablespoon honey
- Ice cubes
- Orange slices and mint leaves for garnish

Directions:

1. In a saucepan, bring water to a gentle boil, then remove from heat.
2. Steep chamomile tea bags in hot water for 5 minutes.
3. Remove the tea bags and stir in honey until fully dissolved.
4. In a pitcher, combine chamomile tea, orange juice, and lemon juice, mix well.
5. Serve over ice, garnished with orange slices and mint leaves.

Nutritional Information:

Calories: 85, Protein: 1g, Carbohydrates: 22g, Fat: 0g, Fiber: 1g, Cholesterol: 0 mg, Sodium: 5 mg, Potassium: 180 mg

SAGE & PEAR REFRESHER

🍽 4 SERVINGS ⏱ 10 MINUTES 🕐 0 MINUTES

Ingredients:

- 4 fresh sage leaves
- 2 ripe pears, peeled and cored
- 1 cup pear juice
- 1 tablespoon lemon juice
- 1 cup sparkling water
- Ice cubes
- Sage sprigs, for garnish

Directions:

1. Combine sage leaves, ripe pears, pear juice, and lemon juice in a blender.
2. Blend until smooth and strain the mixture into a mixing bowl to remove pulp.
3. Divide the strained juice into four glasses filled with ice cubes.
4. Top each glass with sparkling water and stir gently.
5. Garnish with a fresh sage sprig and serve chilled.

Nutritional Information:

Calories: 85, Protein: 1g, Carbohydrates: 22g, Fat: 0g, Fiber: 4g, Cholesterol: 0mg, Sodium: 5mg, Potassium: 195mg

Moctails

THYME PINEAPPLE SPRITZ

🍽 4 SERVINGS　　⏱ 10 MINUTES　　🕔 5 MINUTES

Ingredients:

- 1 cup Fresh Pineapple Juice
- 1/2 cup Water
- 10 sprigs Fresh Thyme
- 2 tablespoons Honey
- 1 cup Sparkling Water
- 1 tablespoon Fresh Lime Juice
- Ice Cubes
- Pineapple Slices and Additional Thyme Sprigs for Garnish

Directions:

1. In a small saucepan, combine water and 8 sprigs of thyme. Bring to a simmer and cook for 5 minutes to make a thyme-infused syrup. Remove from heat and let it cool slightly.
2. Strain the syrup to remove thyme sprigs and stir in honey until fully dissolved.
3. In a cocktail shaker, combine pineapple juice, thyme syrup, lime juice, and a handful of ice cubes. Shake well until chilled.
4. Divide the mixture between four glasses, filling each halfway.
5. Top each glass with sparkling water and garnish with a pineapple slice and a sprig of thyme. Serve immediately.

Nutritional Information:

Calories: 70, Protein: 0g, Carbohydrates: 18g, Fat: 0g, Fiber: 1g, Cholesterol: 0mg, Sodium: 2mg, Potassium: 80mg

HIBISCUS ROSE COOLER

🍽 4 SERVINGS　　⏱ 10 MINUTES　　🕔 5 MINUTES

Ingredients:

- 1 cup dried hibiscus flowers
- 3 cups water
- 2 tablespoons rose water
- 1/4 cup honey (or to taste)
- 1/2 cup freshly squeezed lemon juice
- Lemon slices and fresh mint leaves for garnish

Directions:

1. Heat water in a saucepan over medium heat and bring to a simmer.
2. Add the dried hibiscus flowers to the simmering water and let steep for 5 minutes.
3. Strain the hibiscus mixture into a pitcher, discarding the flowers.
4. Stir in the rose water, honey, and lemon juice until well combined.
5. Chill the mixture in the refrigerator for at least 30 minutes.
6. Serve over ice, garnished with lemon slices and mint leaves.

Nutritional Information:

Calories: 70, Protein: 0g, Carbohydrates: 18g, Fat: 0g, Fiber: 0g, Cholesterol: 0mg, Sodium: 5mg, Potassium: 30mg

Mocktails

EUCALYPTUS LIME TONIC

4 SERVINGS   **10 MINUTES**   **5 MINUTES**

Ingredients:

- 1 tablespoon dried eucalyptus leaves
- 4 cups water
- 1/4 cup lime juice (freshly squeezed)
- 2 tablespoons honey (or to taste)
- 1 cup sparkling water
- Lime slices and eucalyptus sprigs for garnish (optional)

Directions:

1. In a medium saucepan, bring the water to a gentle boil and add the eucalyptus leaves. Simmer for 5 minutes.
2. Remove the saucepan from heat and let the infusion steep for an additional 5 minutes.
3. Strain the infused water through a fine mesh strainer into a pitcher, discarding the leaves.
4. Stir in the lime juice and honey until well combined.
5. Refrigerate the mixture until chilled, about 20 minutes.
6. Just before serving, add the sparkling water to the pitcher.
7. Pour over ice in glasses and garnish with lime slices and eucalyptus sprigs if desired.

Nutritional Information:

Calories: 35, Protein: 0g, Carbohydrates: 9g, Fat: 0g, Fiber: 0g, Cholesterol: 0mg, Sodium: 5mg, Potassium: 15mg

PEPPERMINT PEACH FIZZ

2 SERVINGS   **10 MINUTES**   **0 MINUTES**

Ingredients:

- 1 cup fresh peach slices
- 1/2 cup fresh peppermint leaves
- 1 tablespoon honey (or agave syrup)
- 1 cup sparkling water
- Ice cubes (as needed)
- Fresh mint sprigs, for garnish

Directions:

1. Blend the peach slices and peppermint leaves until smooth in a blender.
2. Strain the mixture through a fine mesh strainer into a mixing glass to remove pulp.
3. Stir in honey and sparkling water until well combined.
4. Fill two serving glasses with ice cubes, then pour the peppermint peach mixture over the ice.
5. Garnish with fresh mint sprigs before serving.

Nutritional Information:

Calories: 80, Protein: 1g, Carbohydrates: 21g, Fat: 0g, Fiber: 2g, Cholesterol: 0mg, Sodium: 10mg, Potassium: 180mg

Moctails

LEMON VERBENA DELIGHT

4 SERVINGS   **10 MINUTES**   **0 MINUTES**

Ingredients:

- 1 cup fresh lemon verbena leaves
- 4 cups water
- 1/2 cup fresh lemon juice
- 2 tablespoons honey
- Ice cubes
- Lemon slices for garnish

Directions:

1. In a large pitcher, combine the lemon verbena leaves and water, allowing the flavors to infuse for 5 minutes.
2. Strain the infused water into a shaker, discarding the leaves.
3. Add the lemon juice and honey to the shaker, then fill with ice.
4. Shake vigorously until well combined and chilled.
5. Strain the mocktail into glasses filled with fresh ice.
6. Garnish each glass with a lemon slice. Serve immediately.

Nutritional Information:

Calories: 45, Protein: 0g, Carbohydrates: 12g, Fat: 0g, Fiber: 0g, Cholesterol: 0 mg, Sodium: 5 mg, Potassium: 55 mg

GINGER LEMONGRASS SPLASH

4 SERVINGS   **10 MINUTES**   **5 MINUTES**

Ingredients:

- 2 stalks lemongrass, chopped
- 1-inch piece of fresh ginger, sliced
- 4 cups water
- 2 tablespoons honey or agave syrup
- 1 tablespoon lime juice
- Ice cubes
- Fresh mint leaves for garnish

Directions:

1. In a small saucepan, bring the water, lemongrass, and ginger to a boil. Reduce heat and simmer for 5 minutes.
2. Remove from heat and strain the mixture into a pitcher, discarding the solids.
3. Stir in the honey or agave syrup until dissolved, then add the lime juice.
4. Fill glasses with ice cubes and pour the ginger lemongrass infusion over the ice.
5. Garnish with fresh mint leaves and serve immediately.

Nutritional Information:

Calories: 30, Protein: 0g, Carbohydrates: 8g, Fat: 0g, Fiber: 0g, Cholesterol: 0 mg, Sodium: 5 mg, Potassium: 25 mg

Mocktails

Mocktails for Kids

FIZZY BERRY LEMONADE

🍽 4 SERVINGS   ⏱ 10 MINUTES   🕐 0 MINUTES

Ingredients:

- 2 cups lemonade
- 1 cup mixed berries (fresh or frozen)
- 1 cup sparkling water
- 1 tablespoon honey (optional)
- Ice cubes for serving
- Fresh mint leaves for garnish

Directions:

1. In a pitcher, add the mixed berries and use a muddler to gently crush them, releasing their juices.
2. Pour in the lemonade and stir well to combine with the berries.
3. Add the sparkling water and gently stir to maintain the fizziness.
4. Taste and optionally add honey for extra sweetness, stirring until dissolved.
5. Fill glasses with ice cubes and pour the fizzy berry lemonade over the top.
6. Garnish each glass with a fresh mint leaf before serving.

Nutritional Information:

Calories: 50, Protein: 1g, Carbohydrates: 12g, Fat: 0g, Fiber: 2g, Cholesterol: 0 mg, Sodium: 5 mg, Potassium: 60 mg

RAINBOW FRUIT PUNCH

🍽 4 SERVINGS   ⏱ 10 MINUTES   🕐 0 MINUTES

Ingredients:

- 1 cup Pineapple Juice
- 1 cup Orange Juice
- 1/2 cup Cranberry Juice
- 1/2 cup Blueberry Juice
- 1/2 cup Lemon-Lime Soda
- 1/2 cup Fresh Mixed Berries (strawberries, blueberries, raspberries)
- Ice Cubes

Directions:

1. In a large pitcher, combine pineapple juice, orange juice, cranberry juice, and blueberry juice.
2. Stir the juices together until well mixed.
3. Add the lemon-lime soda and gently stir to combine.
4. Fill four glasses with ice cubes.
5. Divide the fresh mixed berries among the glasses.
6. Pour the juice mixture over the ice and berries in each glass.
7. Serve immediately and enjoy the burst of fruity colors and flavors.

Nutritional Information:

Calories: 150, Protein: 1g, Carbohydrates: 38g, Fat: 0g, Fiber: 2g, Cholesterol: 0mg, Sodium: 5mg, Potassium: 180mg

Moctails

STRAWBERRY BANANA FIZZ

4 SERVINGS   10 MINUTES   0 MINUTES

Ingredients:

- 1 cup Strawberries, hulled and sliced
- 1 Banana, sliced
- 1 1/2 cups Club Soda
- 1 tablespoon Honey (optional)
- 1/2 cup Ice Cubes
- Fresh Mint Leaves, for garnish

Directions:

1. In a blender, combine the strawberries, banana, and honey (if using). Blend until smooth.
2. Pour the mixture through a strainer into a jug to remove any pulp for a smoother texture.
3. Add the club soda to the jug, stirring gently to combine.
4. Fill each glass halfway with ice cubes, then pour the strawberry banana mixture over the ice.
5. Garnish with fresh mint leaves before serving.

Nutritional Information:

Calories: 58, Protein: 0.6g, Carbohydrates: 14g, Fat: 0.2g, Fiber: 2g, Cholesterol: 0 mg, Sodium: 12 mg, Potassium: 200 mg

COTTON CANDY CLOUD COOLER

4 SERVINGS   10 MINUTES   0 MINUTES

Ingredients:

- 2 cups Sparkling Water
- 1 cup Pink Lemonade
- 1 cup Grape Juice
- 1 tablespoon Cotton Candy Syrup
- 1 cup Ice Cubes
- 1/2 cup Mini Cotton Candy Fluff (for garnish)

Directions:

1. In a blender, combine the sparkling water, pink lemonade, grape juice, and cotton candy syrup.
2. Add the ice cubes and blend until smooth.
3. Pour the mixture into a pitcher and stir gently with a spoon.
4. Divide the cooler into four glasses.
5. Top each glass with a small amount of cotton candy fluff for garnish.

Nutritional Information:

Calories: 85, Protein: 0g, Carbohydrates: 22g, Fat: 0g, Fiber: 0g, Cholesterol: 0 mg, Sodium: 5 mg, Potassium: 60 mg

Moctails

BLUEBERRY BUBBLE MOCKTAIL

4 SERVINGS   10 MINUTES   0 MINUTES

Ingredients:

- 1 cup fresh blueberries
- 2 cups sparkling water
- 1/4 cup lemon juice
- 2 tablespoons honey (or agave syrup for a vegan option)
- Ice cubes
- Fresh mint leaves (for garnish)

Directions:

1. Blend the blueberries in a blender until you achieve a smooth puree.
2. Strain the blueberry puree through a fine mesh strainer into a large pitcher to remove the pulp.
3. Add lemon juice and honey to the blueberry juice in the pitcher, stirring well until combined.
4. Slowly pour in the sparkling water, stirring gently to maintain the bubbles.
5. Fill serving glasses with ice cubes, then pour the blueberry mixture over the ice.
6. Garnish each glass with a sprig of fresh mint before serving.

Nutritional Information:

Calories: 45, Protein: 0.5g, Carbohydrates: 12g, Fat: 0g, Fiber: 2g, Cholesterol: 0mg, Sodium: 10mg, Potassium: 70mg

TROPICAL UNICORN SPRITZ

4 SERVINGS   10 MINUTES   0 MINUTES

Ingredients:

- 1 cup pineapple juice
- 1 cup coconut water
- 1/2 cup frozen mixed berries
- 1/2 cup sparkling water
- 1 tablespoon honey (optional for added sweetness)
- Ice cubes
- Fresh mint leaves for garnish

Directions:

1. Blend the pineapple juice, coconut water, and frozen mixed berries until smooth.
2. Pour the blended mixture into a pitcher.
3. Add the sparkling water and honey, stirring gently to combine.
4. Fill each glass with ice cubes and pour the Tropical Unicorn Spritz over the ice.
5. Garnish with fresh mint leaves and serve immediately to enjoy the colorful delight.

Nutritional Information:

Calories: 60, Protein: 0g, Carbohydrates: 15g, Fat: 0g, Fiber: 1g, Cholesterol: 0 mg, Sodium: 10 mg, Potassium: 150 mg

Moctails

WATERMELON WONDER SPLASH

🍽 4 SERVINGS   ⏱ 10 MINUTES   🕐 0 MINUTES

Ingredients:

- 4 cups fresh watermelon, cubed
- 1 cup coconut water
- 2 tablespoons lime juice
- 1 tablespoon honey (optional, for added sweetness)
- Ice cubes as desired
- Fresh mint leaves for garnish

Directions:

1. Blend watermelon cubes in a blender until smooth.
2. Pour the blended watermelon through a sieve into a pitcher to remove seeds and pulp.
3. Stir in coconut water, lime juice, and honey until well combined.
4. Fill each glass with ice cubes and pour the watermelon mixture over the ice.
5. Garnish with fresh mint leaves and serve immediately.

Nutritional Information:

Calories: 70, Protein: 1g, Carbohydrates: 18g, Fat: 0g, Fiber: 1g, Cholesterol: 0mg, Sodium: 15mg, Potassium: 240mg

CHOCOLATE MILKSHAKE SPRITZER

🍽 2 SERVINGS   ⏱ 10 MINUTES   🕐 0 MINUTES

Ingredients:

- 1 cup chocolate milk
- 1 cup sparkling water
- 2 tablespoons chocolate syrup
- Whipped cream, to garnish
- Chocolate shavings or sprinkles, to garnish

Directions:

1. Combine chocolate milk and chocolate syrup in a blender. Blend until smooth.
2. Divide the mixture evenly into two tall glasses.
3. Slowly pour sparkling water into each glass, stirring gently with a whisk to combine.
4. Top each glass with a dollop of whipped cream.
5. Garnish with chocolate shavings or sprinkles for a fun finish.

Nutritional Information:

Calories: 120, Protein: 3g, Carbohydrates: 24g, Fat: 2g, Fiber: 1g, Cholesterol: 8mg, Sodium: 50mg, Potassium: 250mg

Moctails

APPLE PIE SPARKLE

2 SERVINGS   **10 MINUTES**   **0 MINUTES**

Ingredients:
- 1 cup Apple Juice
- 1 cup Sparkling Water
- 1/2 teaspoon Ground Cinnamon
- 1 tablespoon Honey
- 1/2 cup Ice Cubes
- 2 Apple Slices (for garnish)

Directions:
1. In a blender, combine apple juice, ground cinnamon, honey, and ice cubes. Blend until smooth.
2. Pour the mixture evenly into two tall glasses.
3. Add 1/2 cup of sparkling water to each glass. Stir gently to combine.
4. Garnish with an apple slice on the rim of each glass.
5. Serve immediately and enjoy the fizzy, sweet taste of apple pie!

Nutritional Information:
Calories: 90, Protein: 0g,
Carbohydrates: 24g, Fat: 0g, Fiber: 1g,
Cholesterol: 0 mg, Sodium: 5 mg,
Potassium: 180 mg

KIWI MELON MAGIC

2 SERVINGS   **10 MINUTES**   **0 MINUTES**

Ingredients:
- 2 ripe kiwis, peeled and sliced
- 1 cup honeydew melon, cubed
- 1 tablespoon honey (optional, for extra sweetness)
- 1 cup sparkling water
- Ice cubes (as needed)
- Fresh mint leaves for garnish

Directions:
1. In a blender, combine the kiwi slices, honeydew melon cubes, and honey. Blend until smooth.
2. Strain the mixture to remove seeds, if desired, and pour the juice back into the blender.
3. Add ice cubes to the blender and pulse until the mixture is slushy.
4. Divide the mixture evenly between two serving glasses.
5. Top each glass with sparkling water for a fizzy finish.
6. Garnish with mint leaves and a kiwi slice on the rim of each glass.
7. Serve immediately and enjoy the fresh taste of Kiwi Melon Magic!

Nutritional Information:
Calories: 85, Protein: 1g,
Carbohydrates: 21g, Fat: 0g, Fiber: 3g,
Cholesterol: 0mg, Sodium: 10mg,
Potassium: 280mg

Moctails

GRAPE GALAXY FIZZ

4 SERVINGS   10 MINUTES   0 MINUTES

Ingredients:

- 2 cups Seedless Red Grapes
- 1 cup Chilled Sparkling Water
- 1/2 cup Fresh Orange Juice
- 1 tbsp Honey or Agave Syrup (optional)
- 4 slices Orange (for garnish)
- 1/4 cup Crushed Ice

Directions:

1. Blend the seedless red grapes until smooth. Strain the juice into the pitcher.
2. Add the fresh orange juice and honey or agave syrup to the pitcher. Stir well to combine.
3. Gently stir in the chilled sparkling water to keep the fizz alive.
4. Fill each glass with crushed ice, then pour the grape mixture over the ice.
5. Garnish each drink with a slice of orange for a zesty touch.
6. Serve immediately and let the galaxy of flavors take over!

Nutritional Information:

Calories: 50, Protein: 0.5g, Carbohydrates: 12g, Fat: 0g, Fiber: 1g, Cholesterol: 0mg, Sodium: 5mg, Potassium: 150mg

ORANGE CREAM DREAM

2 SERVINGS   10 MINUTES   0 MINUTES

Ingredients:

- 1 cup orange juice
- 1/2 cup vanilla yogurt
- 1/2 cup ice cubes
- 1 tablespoon honey (optional, for added sweetness)
- 1/4 teaspoon vanilla extract
- Orange slices and a cherry for garnish (optional)

Directions:

1. Combine orange juice, vanilla yogurt, and ice cubes in a blender.
2. Add honey and vanilla extract for extra sweetness and flavor, if desired.
3. Blend on high speed until smooth and creamy.
4. Pour the mixture into tall glasses.
5. Garnish with orange slices and a cherry on top.
6. Serve immediately and enjoy the creamy, dreamy goodness!

Nutritional Information:

Calories: 130, Protein: 4g, Carbohydrates: 26g, Fat: 2g, Fiber: 0g, Cholesterol: 5mg, Sodium: 40mg, Potassium: 350mg

Moctails

Conclusion

Congratulations! You've just taken a delicious dive into the vibrant world of mocktails. From fruity delights to exotic blends and energizing creations, you now have a wealth of recipes at your fingertips. Whether you're hosting a lively gathering or enjoying a quiet evening at home, there's always a mocktail to match the moment.

The beauty of mocktails lies in their endless versatility and creativity. You can mix, match, and experiment with flavors to craft drinks that suit your personal taste. Don't be afraid to swap ingredients, add your own twist, or create signature recipes that reflect your style.

Most importantly, remember that mocktails are more than just drinks — they're an invitation to savor life's small joys. Each sip is an opportunity to celebrate fresh ingredients, share moments with loved ones, and embrace a healthier lifestyle without compromising on flavor or fun.

Thank you for joining me on this journey. May your glasses always be filled with refreshing creations and your moments filled with joy.

Cheers to a new world of flavor — one mocktail at a time!

Index

A

Acai Berry Refresher 43
Alcohol-Free Cosmo Cooler 50
Almond Joy Refresher 57
Aloe Vera Lemon Cooler 28
Apple Cider Spritz 51
Apple Pie Sparkle 71
Avocado Cilantro Smooth Sip 34

B

Banoffee Cream Cooler 55
Basil Berry Bliss 61
Beet Ginger Booster 40
Beetroot Lemon Spritz 35
Berry Burst Bliss 11
Berry Light Sparkler 27
Bloody Mary Mocktail 33
Blueberry Basil Spritzer 16
Blueberry Bubble Mocktail 69

C

Celery Salt & Lemon Fizz 35
Chamomile Citrus Dream 62
Chocolate Milkshake Spritzer 70
Chocolate Mint Bliss 53
Cinnamon Roll Elixir 56
Citrus Cloud Elixir 27
Citrus Sunrise Sparkler 12
Classic Lemon Spritzer 49
Classic Shirley Temple 47
Coconut Cream Delight 58
Coconut Espresso Spark 40
Coconut Lychee Cooler 18
Cotton Candy Cloud Cooler 68
Cranberry Orange Cooler 26
Cucumber Coconut Bliss 22
Cucumber Dill Refresher 32

D

Dragonfruit Dream Spritz 18

E

Espresso Orange Twist 39
Eucalyptus Lime Tonic 64

F

Faux Sangria Sparkle 47
Fizzy Berry Lemonade 67

G

Ginger Lemongrass Splash 65
Ginseng Grapefruit Fizz 42
Grape Galaxy Fizz 72
Grapefruit Basil Bliss 30
Green Tea Citrus Charge 41
Green Tea Lime Sparkle 29
Guarana Berry Bliss 42
Guava Hibiscus Fizz 21

H

Hibiscus Rose Cooler 63
Hibiscus Slim Sip 29

J

Jalapeño Lime Zest 34

K

Key Lime Pie Refresher 54
Kiwi Kiss Refresher 15
Kiwi Melon Magic 71

L

Lavender Lemonade Cooler 60
Lemon Chia Energizer 41
Lemon Verbena Delight 65
Light & Lush Lime Spritz 25
Low-Cal Cucumber Mint Refresher 26

M

Mango Magic Mojito 12
Mango Protein Punch 43
Mango Tamarind Elixir 19
Matcha Mint Cooler 39
Mimosa Mocktail 50
Mint & Honey Elixir 61

N

Nojito (Alcohol-Free Mojito) 48
Non-Alcoholic Margarita 49
Non-Alcoholic Martini Twist 51
Non-Alcoholic Piña Colada 46

O

Orange Cream Dream 72

P

Papaya Mint Mojito 21
Passionfruit Paradise Punch 20
Peach Passion Punch 14
Peppermint Peach Fizz 64
Pickled Cucumber Cooler 37
Pineapple Breeze Mocktail 16
Pineapple Ginger Zest 19
Pineapple Spirulina Zest 44
Pomegranate Power Sip 15

R

Rainbow Fruit Punch 67
Raspberry Chocolate Bliss 57
Raspberry Lime Fizz 14

Rosemary Citrus Sparkler 60

S

S'mores Shake Fizz 58
Sage & Pear Refresher 62
Salted Caramel Spritz 55
Skinny Lemon Ginger Fizz 25
Skinny Peachy Punch 30
Smoky Paprika Citrus Splash 37
Spiced Carrot Ginger Spark 33
Spiced Mango Sunrise 22
Starfruit Citrus Sparkler 23
Strawberry Banana Fizz 68
Strawberry Cheesecake Shake 54
Strawberry Lemonade Splash 13
Sweet Potato Maple Swirl 36

T

Tamarind Tangerine Tonic 23
Thai Basil Lime Cooler 20
Thyme Pineapple Spritz 63
Tiramisu Mocktail 56
Tomato Basil Cooler 32
Tropical Paradise Punch 11
Tropical Unicorn Spritz 69
Turmeric Honey Glow 44
Turmeric Tamarind Tonic 36

V

Vanilla Bean Cream Soda 53
Virgin Mary 48
Virgin Mojito 46

W

Watermelon Mint Delight 28
Watermelon Wonder Cooler 13
Watermelon Wonder Splash 70

Printed in Dunstable, United Kingdom